VIKING
LEGENDS

10 BEST VIKING LEGENDS EVER!

Michael Cox

SCHOLASTIC

Scholastic Children's Books,
Euston House, 24 Eversholt Street
London NW1 1DB

A division of Scholastic Limited
London - New York - Toronto - Sydney - Auckland
Mexico City ~ New Delhi ~ Hong Kong

First published in the UK under the title *Top Ten*
by Scholastic Ltd 1999
This edition published 2009

ISBN 978 1407 10826 1

Printed and bound in the UK by CPI Bookmarque, Croydon, Surrey

10 9 8 7 6 5 4 3

CONTENTS

INTRODUCTION

Imagine it's a long time ago, somewhere in northern Europe. It's late at night and you're sitting by a log fire watching the shadows flicker eerily around the walls of the freezing wooden box you call home. Your bum is as numb as a frost-fairy's flip-flop and your legs are stiffer than a snowman's shoelaces. Outside, a pack of wolves are howling for their supper (*you!*). Further down the valley, the homicidal maniacs you jokingly refer to as your "neighbours" are planning to give you a painful (and totally fatal) duffing up the very next morning! "Yes!" you think to yourself, as you listen to an avalanche flattening your best cow shed; "Life isn't exactly a bundle of laughs at the moment!"

Then a member of your family begins to spin a terrific tale of powerful gods, fearless heroes, troublesome giants and moronic monsters. In no time at all, you're appalled by its scenes of gruesome gore, rendered helpless with laughter by its fantastic humour and awestruck by its wisdom. And, when this staggering story – or legend, as we now call it – has reached its riveting conclusion, you feel about a billion times better.

Legends were common throughout the ancient world. As well as entertaining people they helped them make sense of the confusing and hostile world around them. The ten thrilling legends in this book are all about the adventures of the gang of gods who were worshipped by people who lived in Norway, Sweden and Denmark (Scandinavia) and Iceland during the time before Christianity came to northern Europe. In other words ... the Vikings! Throughout the time that the Vikings, or "ancient Norse", ruled the roost – approximately AD 750-1050 (give or take the odd pillaging trip) – they found their legends tremendously inspiring. Believing in their gods and superheroes and hearing stories of how they sorted out their problems, reassured them and gave them the confidence to "bash on regardless" (in more ways than one!). As for all sorts of people at all sorts of times in history, their religious beliefs were very important to them and gave them the courage to face an uncertain future.

Most Vikings didn't have time for swotty stuff like reading and writing because they were far too busy living action-packed lives. And dying action-packed deaths! They passed on the legends by telling them to each other or hearing them as poems from story-tellers known as skalds and bards. Fortunately for us, around the time that Christianity was fast becoming the flavour of the millennium in northern Europe and the Norse gods and goddesses were losing their popularity, two Scandinavian scholars decided to write some of the Viking legends down before they were all forgotten. One of them was an Icelander called Snorri Sturluson. Snorri thought the legends were fun and he realized that the people who had made them up had a vivid imagination and a great sense of humour! He called his two collections of legends the Prose Edda and the Poetic Edda.

So, thanks to Snorri and a few other Scandinavian swots, here are ten of the very best Viking legends ever told. They've been brought up to date and linked with fantastic fact sections so that you'll know a bit more about the sort of world they took place in. We can't guarantee that they've had *all* the gruesome bits removed but they're *reasonably* wholesome now.

Well! What are you waiting for? Give the reindeer an extra bale of hay, throw a couple of logs on the fire, bolt the front door ... and curl up with the ten best Viking Legends ... ever!

LEGEND 1: THE CREATION

The world as it exists today is a complicated and mind-boggling place isn't it? And trying to imagine how it all got going in the first place is definitely the sort of thing that is guaranteed to make your brains dribble out of your ears if you think about it for more than five minutes at a time. Nevertheless, the riddle of how the world was created, not to mention lots of other questions like "Who did it?" and, "Why?" and "Did they ever take tea breaks?" has been puzzling human beings for almost as long as they've been around. Over the centuries people have come up with all sorts of amazing explanations ranging from the Christian Bible version as told in Genesis to the latest "Big Bang" theory favoured by modern scientists. The Vikings had a few ideas of their own about how the world began and their explanation of how things all got started provides our first legend. Some experts might disagree with one or two of the scientific "facts" in this legend but it's definitely imaginative, action-packed, colourful … and extremely entertaining! So here, in ten easy-to-follow steps, is the Viking version of the Big Bang theory…

The "Big Drip" theory: how the world began

One In the beginning there was nothing at all but a huge empty space which was absolutely bursting at the seams with vast, incredibly empty (and excruciatingly boring) amounts of … NOTHING! All this nothingness was called Ginnungagap. On the northern side of Ginnungagap there was a land of ice and snow and mists called Niflheim and on the southern side was a land of flames and sparks called Muspell.

Two Eventually, with much bad tempered hissing, spluttering and steaming, the ice and fire from the two lands began to mix. As the flames roared and the melting ice poured into Ginnungagap a giant man rose up out of the steam. He was enormous – his underpants alone would probably have been big enough to contain the entire population of modern Europe. This "big drip" of a giant, whose name was Ymir, was said to be the very first living being ever. But sadly, he was also extremely EVIL!

Three Ymir had numerous and totally disgusting personal problems, one of which was sweating a lot as he slept. One day (and no doubt much to his surprise) some of the smelly great globules of greasy gunk that dribbled from his oozing armpits turned into a fully grown giant man and woman. Some people sweat "buckets", some people sweat "cobs" ... Ymir went one better – he sweated "*giants*"!

Four Meanwhile, lower down his body, Ymir's legs (obviously not wishing to be outdone by his armpits) got together and produced a giant of their own. This *leg-end*ary monster had six heads and went by the name of Thrudgelmir. Thrudgelmir eventually had a one-headed son called Bergelmir. Bergelmir was said to be the grand-daddy of all frost giants, the huge icy-cold beings who were soon to become the all-time enemies of the gods.

Frost Giants

Five Things were beginning to happen all over the place now! Some of the melted ice from Ginnungagap turned into an enormous cow called Audumla and four rivers of milk began to flow from her udder. Ignoring the fact that it was probably full of millions of harmful bacteria and unhealthy calories, greedy Ymir drank gallons and gallons of it.

Audumla

Six While Ymir was getting into some serious dairy product abuse, Audumla kept herself alive by licking at a salty block of ice. After three days of non-stop licking a living man popped out of the ice-block. He was called Buri and he became the forefather of all of the gods.

Seven Time passed and Buri had a son called Bor. The two of them began to fight a war with the evil frost giants which went on for ages and ages and ages (so long that many of the giants became completely *Bor*ed to death!). The frost giants kept on producing lots of (not so) little frost giant children of their own who joined in the war as soon as they were big enough (which didn't take long at all).

Eight Despite the fact that he was fighting a savage war with the frost giants (and possibly in a moment of rather embarrassing absentmindedness) Bor married a frost giantess called Bestla and they had three sons called Odin, Vili and Ve. The three brothers absolutely hated all the frost giants especially enormous, sweaty, evil

Ymir. So one day they murdered the big pudding. Great torrents of blood poured from his body and drowned all of the frost giants (ha ha!), apart from Bergelmir and his wife. The brothers were also safe, because they'd had the sense to build a boat from a tree trunk and were able to float around in the blood for a bit while they decided what to do next.

Nine The brothers (who were obviously keen environmentalists) were anxious not to waste one single bit of big Ymir's body so they decided to recycle it. This is what they did with him:

They raised Ymir's skull into the air and made the sky from it but had to employ four dwarves to hold up a corner each to prevent it from crashing down.

They threw his brains up in the air and they immediately became the clouds. (Don't say you hadn't noticed!)

They used his unbroken bones to create the mountains.

They threw his body into Ginnungap where his flesh became the Earth that we all live on today.

They made his teeth and jaws and his broken bones into the rocks and boulders.

They used his blood to make the rivers and lakes and a huge ocean which completely surrounded the land.

Ten Give or take a few finishing touches, the world of the humans was now more or less finished – all it needed was some *people* to put in it. This didn't take Odin, Vili and Ve long at all to sort out (well, they *were* gods!). One day when they were out jogging along the seashore they came across a couple of fallen trees – one was an ash and the other was an elm.

"Hmm!" they all said thoughtfully. "These trees would make really neat human beings wouldn't they?"

And, quick as a flash, they turned the trees into the first proper human beings in the whole world! They made the ash tree into a man called Ask and the elm tree into a woman called Embla. Every single person in the whole world – and this includes *you* reader – is descended from these two people.

So now you know the truth – and it couldn't be simpler: your family tree actually began … as a couple of trees!

FANTASTIC FACTS 1: A ROUGH GUIDE TO THE WORLD OF THE VIKING LEGENDS

The world of the Viking legends can be a pretty complicated place to find your way around – especially if you are a newcomer. All sorts of horrors and dangers lurk around every corner. So, before setting out to meet the weird and wonderful characters who live in it, it might be a good idea to get to know some of its main districts ... just so you aren't caught unawares!

The handy picture map on the next page will help you. Please note – the distances between locations aren't to scale. Please allow anything between five minutes ... and five thousand years for your journeys!

1 The nine worlds

A few important words of explanation before we begin our rough guided tour. The world (or universe) of the Norse legends was actually said to be made up of the nine different worlds which you are going to read about. What with written versions of the legends being thin on the ground (not to mention them all being entirely fictitious in the first place!) no one is completely sure what or where the nine worlds all were. For the purpose of most of the legends it's easiest to think of them as follows: Asgard; Midgard; Jotunheim; Vanaheim; Nidavellir; Svartalfheim; Alfheim; and Niflheim. That's it ... give or take Muspell and Hel! (If you find this confusing, imagine what it must have been like for the taxi drivers and postmen!)

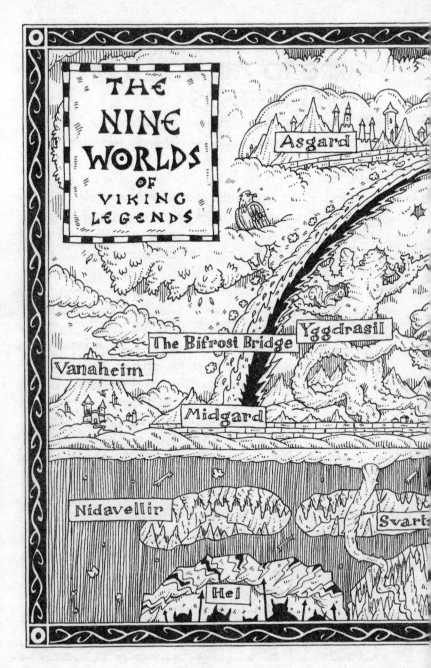

THE
NINE
WORLDS
OF
VIKING
LEGENDS

Asgard

The Bifrost Bridge

Yggdrasil

Vanaheim

Midgard

Nidavellir

Svarta

Hel

2 Asgard

Asgard is the home (or world) of the gods. It is an extremely upmarket and well fortified neighbourhood and is situated high above Midgard, the next stop on our tour. It is full of green, open spaces and posh, shiny palaces made from precious metals and stones. These imposing residences provide the sort of first class accommodation that all gods are accustomed to.

3 Midgard

Midgard is sometimes called the Middle World. The gods fortified it with a big wall which they made out of Ymir's eyebrows. After they had created the first man and woman (Ask and Embla) they gave them Midgard to live in – completely rent-free! (Obviously they were feeling in a generous mood.) From that day on it became the world of all human beings (so you'll probably feel quite at home here).

4 Jotunheim

Jotunheim is the land (or world) that was given to the giants by Odin after the Creation. It is situated between the edge of the ocean and Midgard, and is full of rocks, ice and not much else. (Definitely no palm trees or white sandy beaches!) It's the sort of place that macho types like the god Thor (and PE teachers) go to test their strength and prove their limitless courage. The frost giant Bergelmir and his wife landed up here after they'd survived the great blood flood, so they settled down and energetically set about producing lots of rock and frost giant children who would go on to be a constant nuisance to the gods and humans.

5 Niflheim, Hel and Muspell

Niflheim and Hel are part of the underworld and they are very unpleasant places indeed. No one is actually sure whether they are two entirely separate worlds or if Hel is just a suburb of Niflheim. What we can be sure of is that they are more or less next door to each other. So … if someone stops and asks you for directions to Niflheim it is perfectly OK to say, "Go to Hel!" Muspell is the land of fire and flame just around the corner from Niflheim.

6 Vanaheim

Vanaheim was the land (or world) of the family of gods known as the Vanir. The Vanir were peaceful gods who enjoyed things like farming and fishing. After they'd had a bit of a falling out with the warlike family of gods known as the Aesir, then made friends again, quite a few of the Vanir sold up and went to live with them in Asgard. As a result, Vanaheim and the Vanir generally get much less of a mention in the legends than Asgard and the Aesir. Which makes sense doesn't it! After all, legends about successful carrot harvests and caterpillar management programmes aren't going to be half as exciting as scintillating sagas of savagery and skullduggery, are they?

7 Nidavellir, Svartalfheim and Alfheim

These are the three worlds where the elves and the dwarves live. You'll find out more about them in legend **5**.

8 Gladsheim

Gladsheim, not one of the worlds itself, but an extremely luxurious palace in Asgard which acts as a sort of five-star conference hall and management training centre for the gods. Whenever there is a crisis on or any big decisions have to be taken they meet here, have a mass chin-wag, consolidate their team spirit, then go out into the worlds and kick giants (or whoever else happens to have been daft enough upset them)!

9 Yggdrasil

Yggdrasil is the meganormous tree that spans the entire universe of the Viking legends. Asgard is in its topmost branches, Midgard surrounds its trunk and the Netherworld (Underworld) is below it. (It would be, wouldn't it?) It has three huge roots which reach all the way into Niflheim, Asgard and Jotunheim. There is always a squirrel running up and down its trunk and a hawk and an eagle sitting in its branches. It is said that this great tree will be around for ever (well, at least until someone replaces it with an out of town shopping centre).

10 The Bifrost Bridge

The Bifrost Bridge is the main thoroughfare that connects Asgard (Heaven) to Midgard (Earth). It is said to be made from red fire, green water and blue air and is also called the Rainbow Bridge. There is no charge for using the bridge but Thor, the Viking thunder god, isn't allowed to cross it because it is feared that the thunderbolts that are forever fizzing out of his massive feet might cause severe structural damage to this important crossing place. As a result he is made to go the long way round whenever he feels like paying a visit to Midgard or anywhere else in the worlds.

LEGEND 2: THE BUILDING OF ASGARD'S WALL

As you've already discovered, some time after the world was made, the two families of gods, the Aesir and the Vanir, had a bit of a quarrel and went to war. Eventually it became obvious that no one would ever win this battle so the families made friends and peace was declared. Unfortunately the war left the wall around Asgard looking rather the worse for wear and it remained like this for many years to come as the gods weren't too keen on getting their hands dirty or becoming involved in undignified and ungodlike activities like DIY. This did leave them at a bit of a disadvantage because without their wall they were wide open to attack by aggressive types like frost and rock giants. Sooner or later, something would have to be done! The second legend in our ten best ever concerns the rebuilding of the wall and the problems that it brought. It's told by Freyja, the goddess of love, who may well have been rather annoyed by the male gods' reluctance to do anything about the terrible state of their defences.

Hi y'all! I'm Freyja. I'm the Norse Goddess of Love and the daughter of the sea god Njord. I'm also generally considered to be rather good looking. Well to be honest, completely "drop dead gorgeous" even if I do say so myself.

ME!

I want to tell you the tale of our wall. The whole thing was a very odd business all round ... and more to the point, yours truly was right in the middle of it — the story that is, not the wall!

Quite soon after the Creation, the gods began falling out something rotten. You know what chaps are like, don't you — always having to prove they're tougher than the next bloke. Talk about a non-stop punch up — they were all at it like cat and god for ages! Nothing but a bunch of overgrown schoolgods if you ask me!

After a while — when they were all completely worn out — things settled down a bit. But by this time, the nice big wall around Asgard was in ruins.

Which wasn't surprising really, what with them slamming each other's heads against it every five minutes! And it wasn't as though we could do without it either — we needed its protection against marauding giants and monsters and the like! But those good for nothing gods just wouldn't lift a finger to put it right!

"If I've asked you lot once I've asked you a thousand times!" I would say to them. "Just when are you going to get round to rebuilding that wall!?"

But the only reply I ever got was, "Hark at her, she's off again! REBUILD THE WALL! CLEAN THE BLOCKED FJORD! DEFROST THE TUNDRA! FIX THAT SAGGING CONTINENTAL SHELF! MEND THAT DRIPPING GLACIER! She never stops!"

Then just when I was beginning to despair of ever seeing the wall put right, the mysterious "builder" turned up. He wandered into Asgard as if he hadn't a care in the world. Humming like an overactive buzz saw, gazing around at the devastation, and

stopping every few minutes
to hitch up his trousers.
They were those special
builder's ones — you know
the sort don't you, forever
slipping down and showing
the top of his bum. It was a very
BIG bum too — well, actually, it was a
GINORMOUS bum! In fact, he was an
extremely BIG chap all over.... he looked
like a very capable fellow indeed.

"Yer wall could do with a bit of a tidy
up, lads," he called to the gods.

"Complete rebuild, if you ask me, mate,"
replied Odin, our top god.

"Well in that case, MATE... I'M
yer man!" said the builder.

"Do you reckon you're up to it?"
asked Loki, a god who doesn't
miss a trick.

ODIN.

"Yup!" says the stranger. "Me and
my horse'll have it sorted in
LOKI a jiffy!"

And then he did a piercing
whistle. Next moment this huge
stallion came galloping up,
snorting and stamping and dropping
great dollops of rhubarb fertilizer

all over the place.

"Hmm, looks promising!" says Odin, sizing up the builder and his nag. "So, what do you want for the job then?"

"Her over there!" said the builder, pointing at ... me! "The blondey one with the big blue eyes and the teeth like glacier mints! I want to marry her!"

I couldn't believe my ears. I was speechless — you could have knocked me down with a fir tree!

"But SHE'S Freyja, the goddess of love!" said Odin.

"Yup, that's the babe I've set my heart on!" said the builder, bold as brass.

"He wants to marry ... FREYJA!" gasped all the other gods.

"You don't want MUCH, do you?" chipped in Loki, sarcastic as ever. "I suppose you'll be asking for the Sun and Moon next!"

"Well ... funnily enough," grinned the builder, "That's PRECISELY what I was going to ask for. My exact price for the job is Freyja, AND the Sun AND the Moon! But there'll be no hidden extras — I promise!

Odin and Loki and the other gods

got together and had a bit of a natter then a few moments later Odin called the builder over and said, "You've got yourself a deal! But on two conditions!"

"Which are," continued Loki, all slimy like, "that you build the wall twice as big as it used to be and finish the job in six months. Otherwise, you don't get paid... not a sausage!"

"Phew... YOU'RE asking a bit much ain't you?" said the builder.

"We could say just the same about you?" said Loki.

"Our terms reflect the hard commercial realities of the world we live in today. Well, that's what HE says." added Odin, pointing to Loki. "So take them or leave them, builder!"

"Oooh, I reckon me and Svaldifari here can manage it," said the builder patting his horse on the bottom and giving me the cheeky eye again. "We'll get cracking right away!"

"Thanks a bunch Loki," I said, as the enormous builder and his super-nag started shifting rubble like they hadnt a second to lose (which they hadnt).

"I don't suppose it occurred to you to ask ME whether I fancied getting hitched to old hippopotamus bottom over there in the first place?"

"Listen Freyja!" whispered Loki "You've nothing to worry about! He'll NEVER finish it on time! It's almost impossible for one man and a horse to rebuild a wall that big in such a short time. But he IS a very handy looking fellow... so they're bound to make progress! I reckon we should get, ooh, at least half the wall built for absolutely nothing at all!

"I just hope you're right?" I said.

Making progress wasn't the half of it — talk about graft! That builder and his horse were like a HUNDRED normal workers. After three months they'd got half of the wall rebuilt. After five months there were only a couple of hundred metres to go! And it wasn't just a case of piling on the rubble and hoping for the best. The whole job was beautifully done. That bloke was a real craftsman — big bum or NO big bum! And that horse of his was something else! Talk about strong! Thor, the god of thunder, was WELL impressed. "Now that's what I call HORSE

POWER!" he said one day, as we watched it pull a couple of tons of boulders up a steep hillside ... with its teeth!

Anyway, with just one week to go and only the main gateway to complete, it was beginning to look like yours truly was going to be sharing her breakfast cornflakes with the builder for quite some time to come — not to mention the whole world being plunged into endless darkness after Mrs Sun and Mr Moon were handed over! We were all horrified!

Then it happened. Just when it looked like all was lost, the builder turned up for work with a face longer than a hungry wolf's death list. It was obvious what the problem was straight away — he hadn't got his horse with him anymore, and he was none too happy about it. And, try as he might, without the wonder-horse he just couldn't make the pace. He grunted, he groaned, he sweated and he cursed (boy did he curse!) but no matter how much he struggled it soon became obvious that he was going to miss his deadline. With just the gateway to finish, his time ran out. And that was when the showdown took place.

"Sorry, builder," piped up Odin. "Time's up and the job ain't finished, so..."
"But it's ALMOST done," protested the builder.

31

"There's only the entrance to finish. Surely you can let me off that. After all I have just built you two thousand kilometres of ten-metre-high wall in just six months!"

"Minus the gateway!" said Odin, "Nothin' doin' bud!"

"I tell you what," pleaded the builder. "I'll just take Freyja and the Sun. You can keep the Moon as a penalty forfeit!"

"Listen broccoli brains, a deal's a deal!" snapped Odin. "So get lost!"

At this point things took an ugly turn with Odin and the builder arguing the toss and all the other gods murmuring and scowling. That's when rootin' tootin' Thor stepped in.

"Just a minute, Dad," he murmured, gently pushing Odin aside. "I think this situation calls for some of my well known tact and subtle charm." And with that, he gave the builder an almighty great smack in the mouth.

That's when the builder revealed his true identity. With a roar of rage he tore off his baseball cap and overalls. And it was immediately plain for all to see that he was a ......
FROST GIANT! Actually, I'd suspected something like that all along, him being the size of a sixteen bedroom farmhouse.

The other gods immediately began

chanting "FIGHT! FIGHT! FIGHT!" as the two of them began to slug it out, deaf to MY cries of "Mind that wall!" Before things could go much further, Odin cried, "Here Thor, catch!" and slung him Mjollnir, his trusty war hammer. Thor caught the super-hammer with his free hand and immediately gave the giant a massive wallop on the bonce with it. Big-bum crashed to the ground — dead as a door knob!

So that was that. We'd got our wall rebuilt for nothing, a dangerous frost giant was dead, the Sun and Moon were still in place and I wasn't going to have to share my duvet with a backside the size of Lapland!

Now, I suppose you're wondering where Svaldifari, the horse, went to. As a matter of fact I didn't find this out until quite a few months later when I asked Loki if he knew anything about it. And naturally, he did!

"When us gods realized that it was looking like we'd have to come up with the payment — that is, you, the Sun and the Moon," said Loki, "we began to get worried. The last thing we wanted was to lose the light of our lives."

"That was very nice of you all to think of me like that," I said.

"I was talking about the Sun and Moon, actually!" said Loki. "Anyway, more to the point, the other gods all began to blame me as I'd set up the deal. So I

decided to make use of my ability to turn
into any shape I choose. Now, I thought,
what sweet little thing would that big,
sweaty stallion find irresistible?"

"Err...a sugar lump?" I suggested.

"No Freyja!" said Loki. "I turned myself into
the cutest little girl pony you ever did
see.   "Then I cantered up to the woods
            where the giant and his horse
            were collecting timber for the
            wall. I pranced about giving
Svadilfari the eye, twitching my withers
and letting him have the occasional flash
of fetlock. He just couldn't take his eyes
off me. Finally, with a toss of his
mane, he pulled his bridle out of the
builder's hand and next moment,
the two of us were galloping up
the mountain side, eager for a spot of
heavy nuzzling followed by some
energetic...."

"Horseplay?" I suggested.

"Exactly!" replied Loki, with a wink.

So readers — that's why the builder
turned up for work without his horse. I
suppose you could say that I got the
story straight from the horse's mouth!

That's about the end of my story —
- apart from one last twist in this
horse's tale. Remember I said that I didn't
get Loki's side of the story until some time
after the whole event. Well, that's because
after him and Svadilfari had galloped off
into the hills, he was gone for months
and months. Then, just when we'd almost

given up hope of seeing him again, he came wandering into Asgard leading the most adorable little foal you ever did see.

"So who's this then?" said Odin, patting the little creature's head.

"This is Sleipnir," said Loki proudly. "My little boy!"

"Your little..... BOY?!" said me and Odin, somewhat amazed.

"Well, my little.... foal, actually!" said Loki. "He's the outcome of my little romance with Sradilfari. When I was more horse shape than god shape."

"Wow!" we both gasped. "You certainly are one versatile sort of a god, Loki!"

"If you want him, Odin, he's yours!" said Loki, handing the reins to Odin.

I could see that Odin was greatly taken with Sleipnir. Especially his FOUR extra legs (something you don't often get on your average horse).

So without hesitation he said, "Thanks Loki. I'd like him very much!"

Odin's never regretted that decision. Sleipnir really has proved to be a gift from a god. He can outrun any horse in the world and also has the remarkable ability to take Odin to the Land of the Dead and back again. What's more, he can gallop across water and fly through the air. A real all purpose, go anywhere horse if ever there was one!

That really is the end of my story. I've got to stop now anyway. I'm beginning to feel a little hoarse.

FANTASTIC FACTS 2: THE GALLERY OF THE GODS

The Viking gods were different from the gods of most other religions because they didn't live for ever. Although the Vikings believed that their gods had great powers and could perform all sorts of miracles, they also thought that they were mortal – just like humans! Their gods were vulnerable to danger, grew old (extremely slowly, with the help of magic), fell out with each other, made stupid mistakes and were finally destroyed by their enemies. In other words they were quite similar to the Vikings themselves in many ways. Here are ten of the top Viking gods. Who's your favourite? The list isn't in any particular order of importance and doesn't include the two top gods, Odin and Thor because they've got their own sections on pages 56 and 73.

1 Freyr

Freyr was the extremely handsome Norse god of good weather and sunshine. His dad was Njord, who was the god of the seas and the wind (weather sort). They both belonged to the family of gods known as the Vanir and were originally brought to Asgard as hostages during the Aesir versus Vanir war along with Freyr's sister Freyja. When the war finally ended they all decided to stay in Asgard.

Freyr's chosen method of transport was a chariot pulled by two huge wild pigs but he also liked to dash around sitting astride a giant wild boar called Gullinbursti. He travelled the seas in a folding ship called Skidbladnir. More about these two later. He was the proud owner of a brilliant magic sword that fought on its own when necessary. This came in really useful if someone was giving him lots of aggro but he wasn't in the mood for a scrap. His other post of special responsibility was ruling over Alfheim, the land of elves and fairies.

2 Freyja

Freyja was Freyr's twin sister and she was the most beautiful of all the goddesses. She was the goddess of love and fertility and was married to a god called Odur. She travelled around in a chariot pulled by a couple of cats and also kept lots of pet cats in her palace. Freyja always wore a fantastic necklace called Brisingamen which was given to her by the dwarves in return  for some snogs and cuddles and whatnot. She also had a cloak made from falcons' feathers which gave her the ability to fly. (This sort of thing only works for Norse gods so put that budgie down this minute!) The Vikings thought so much of Freyja that they named a day of the week after her. Hence the well known saying, "Thank goddess it's Freyjaday!"

3 Frigga

Frigga was sometimes known as Frigg. She was the top goddess and also the queen of all the Aesir. She was the daughter of Odin and Jord. When she grew up she got married to Odin (yes her dad! – Norse gods are allowed do that sort of thing). Her palace was called Fensalir and was a sort of heavenly reunion home for married human couples who'd really  missed each other after one of them died down on earth. Once they had been reunited in Fensalir they could rest assured that they would stay together for evermore (which could be very inconvenient if they suddenly happened to go off each other). She always had a bunch of house keys hanging from her belt to let everyone know that she was a good housewife and was connected with all things homely. She also had the power to make her clothes change from light to dark. She had eleven handmaidens who helped her to spin golden thread and to weave multicoloured clouds on a huge jewel-encrusted spinning wheel. She was the mum of Balder and Hod who were both a bit of a worry to her.

4 Balder

Balder was the son of Odin and Frigga. He was wise, good-looking and kind and never thought a bad thought in his whole life. He was married to Nanna (the Norse goddess of plants … *not* his gran!). He was really good

at reading and writing the
mysterious symbols known
as runes and was also able to
cure all sorts of illnesses using
herbs. He lived in a fab palace
called Breidablik which had a
golden roof supported by silver
pillars. It was said that no lies
could ever get past its doors (so
Balder and Nanna were never
troubled by double glazing firms
or second hand car salesmen).

Balder's twin brother was the blind god called Hod who
was generally thought to be a bit of a baddy.

5 Heimdall

Heimdall was the watchman of
the gods and the god of light.
He guarded Bifrost Bridge and
could see for a hundred miles
by night or day (even further
than that when he'd got his
contact lenses in). His father
was Odin and his mothers were
nine giantesses who Odin sort of
"bumped into" on the beach one
day. The gods chose Heimdall

as bridge-keeper and security-god for Asgard because
of his brill' eyes and ears. His hearing was said to be
so sharp that he could hear the wool growing on the
sheep in Midgard (and a mouse burp at ten thousand
kilometres). They gave him a horn called Gjall which

he was supposed to blow when he saw trouble approaching. Heimdall once had his sword stolen by Loki, the next god on our list.

6 Loki

Although Loki was the son of two giants he really surprised his parents by exceeding their wildest expectations and becoming the Norse god of firesides and relaxation. He was also generally known as the Trickster and the Wizard of Lies because of his mischievous pranks and wicked deeds. Despite the fact that he occasionally did good things, was often quite charming and had a great sense of humour, he was actually a very dodgy character indeed (as you'll discover). He was responsible for bringing about all sorts of chaotic and disastrous situations. He was also able change himself into more or less any shape he wanted to! Fly, seal, salmon, old woman … you name it, he became it! He blamed his love of mischief-making on his intense dislike of being bored (remind you of anyone?). Loki was definitely the sort of god that you'd never buy a second-hand fjord from – or you'd certainly live to regret it!

7 Tyr

Tyr was the son of Odin and Frigga and he was the Norse god of war, fighting and rough stuff in general. The aggro-crazy Vikings thought the world of him and they would often "burst into Tyrs" at tricky bits in battles, yelling his name over and over again in order to give themselves limitless courage (and really sore throats). Many of them had his name written on their sword blades (so that they wouldn't forget who to shout for?). Tyr spent much of his time in Asgard feeding large chunks of raw meat to Loki's  son, the giant wolf called Fenrir (see page 134). The Vikings showed their respect for Tyr by naming a day after him – "Tyrsday" which we now call Tuesday.

8 The Norns

The Norns were three sister goddesses who had control over the future of absolutely everyone else in the world. As a result the other gods often went to them for guidance and advice.

URD · VERDANDI · SKULD

41

Urd was the oldest Norn and she controlled the past. She was forever looking over her shoulder at things that had already happened (and wondering what had caused her incredibly stiff neck). Verdandi was the youngest Norn and she never looked over her shoulder because she was the Norn of the present who faced up to the "here and now" without fear or misgiving. Urd and Verdandi were generally thought to be quite caring and considerate towards humans and gods. The most troublesome Norn was Skuld who was the Norn of the Future. She had special knowledge about what was going to happen and didn't give two hoots for the well-being of either men or gods.

The three Norns spent each day weaving the Web of Fate that affects the destiny of every single god, giant dwarf and human being in the world (including *you*, reader!). Skuld, the most unreliable and unpredictable of the three, was forever unravelling her two sisters' handiwork. The result of this was that no one was ever entirely sure what their future would bring. In other words she was a real "Norn in the side" to everyone, especially TV weather forecasters. (*Tip*: Next time you do badly in a spelling test just tell your teacher that you were powerless to do anything about it as it was all the doing of the Norns.)

The other job of the Norns was to look after Yggdrasil the world tree by pruning it regularly and making sure that its roots were firmly bedded in top quality potting compost.

9 Ran

Ran was the goddess of storms and she lived under the sea with her husband Aegir and their nine daughters. When Viking ships capsized Ran caught drowning sailors in her enormous net and dragged them down to her palace on the sea bed where they were wined and dined and generally well looked after.

The Viking seafarers had such an expert knowledge of the ocean that they were able to identify nine different kinds of waves. And of course, having an expert knowledge of their gods as well, they realized that each of Ran's nine daughters was responsible for causing each different sort of wave. These nine daughters were actually the same women with whom Odin romped in the sand during one of their "out of ocean" paddling sessions – in other words, they were Heimdall's mums … and Ran was his gran!

It was common knowledge that Ran loved gold, so Viking sailors regularly made sure they were carrying some when they set out on a voyage … just in case they happened to have a run in with Ran!

10 Bragi

Bragi was the Norse god of music and poetry. His dad was Odin and his mum was Gunnlod the giantess. He was married to Idun, the goddess of eternal youth. He was the singer-songwriter of the Norse gods and spent his days wandering around playing his magic harp and composing songs to honour dead Vikings who'd been brave in battle (the  wimps were just given a big raspberry). Odin is said to have carved magic writing on Bragi's tongue. This may well have helped the lad with his career as a composer.

LEGEND 3: THE MEAD OF POETRY

Do you enjoy poetry? Most people do … even if it's only the simple sort that's found in the words of most pop songs and birthday cards! It's strange stuff isn't it? It has the power to amuse you, soothe you … or confuse you! But where did it come from in the first place? No one really knows for sure. One thing that legends sometimes attempt to do is to make sense of things that are otherwise a bit of a mystery to us … like poetry! The legend that is usually known as the Mead of Poetry was the ancient Norse way of explaining why some people are born with a gift for producing a sublime rhyme whilst others can only manage a twitty ditty which is just a pity. Odin played a big part in bringing poetry into the world – well, he would wouldn't he? After all, amongst all his other jobs, he *was* the god of poetry. We sent investigative reporter, Vi King, to interview the great god himself. After she'd reassured him that her tape recorder wasn't some diabolical contraption that would steal his soul or turn him into a pillar of cheese he gave her this exclusive interview for legend number three.

The gift of the gob

Vi King: Tell me Odin, how did this whole poetry thing get started in the first place?

Odin: Well, us gods had been knocking seven bells out of each other for quite some time but we finally decided to declare peace. To make our truce official we all got round a table and...

Vi King: Signed a treaty?

Odin: No! We had a mass *spitting* session. By the time we'd finished we'd got a bowl full of the stuff. It was quite good fun actually!

Vi King: Uuurgh ... you disgusting lot!

Odin: Anyway, we'd got this big basin full of saliva and we thought, "Well, seeing as it's here, we might as well turn it into a man!"

Vi King: The way you do?

Odin: Exactly! So we did. We called him Kvasir. He

turned out to be a real treasure. He was wise, thoughtful, patient, understanding and absolutely brilliant with words. He really had got the gift of the gob.

Vi King: The *gob*?

Odin: Sorry, I mean the *gab*! Folk were forever going to him with their personal problems. He always gave them useful advice – often in the form of witty rhymes and ditties. You know the sort of thing: Roedeer are red … icebergs are blue … your foot's in an ice-hole … what should you do?

Vi King: Take off your shoe?

Odin: I haven't a clue. Anyway – this pair of really evil dwarves called Fjalar and Galar got to hear about Kvasir. They said "We want some of that poetic wisdom stuff for ourselves!" and invited good, kind and trusting Kvasir to tea in their cavern. And then – when he was least expecting it – they *liquidated* him!

Vi King: What, killed him?

Odin: Yes, that too! They did that first and *then* they liquidated him.

Vi King: You mean they turned him into liquid?

Odin: Yes, in a way they did! After they'd run him through with their nasty little daggers they dangled him above a big wooden barrel so that all of his blood drained into it. Then they mixed it with honey so that could make…

Vi King: Some mead?

Odin: Yes, apparently they were very keen home brewers. But this particular mead was very, very special because anyone who drank it immediately got instant "poetry power" and also became wise and terrifically knowledgeable .

Vi King: Amazing! You haven't by any chance got any, have you?

Odin: As a matter of fact I have, but that's what this story's all about, isn't it? Anyway, one day the frost giant Gilling and his wife came to visit the dwarves. Quite soon the four of them began to quarrel as these types often do and the deadly duo decided that it was time to be killing the Gillings so they took Mr G for a boat ride and dumped him in the sea. Then they went back to the cave and dropped a millstone on Mrs G's head.

Vi King: Which no doubt gave her a bit of a headache?

Odin: She didn't actually say so – she was dead at the time. After a while the Gilling's son, Suttung, turned up at the dwarves' place and said, "Where are my folks?

What you done with them?" "Erm, we sort of … erm …, *murdered* them." said the dwarves.

Vi King: I bet he was furious.

Odin: He was. He picked up the dwarves by the scruffs of their necks, waded out to a tiny island in the ocean and dumped them on it saying, "When the tide comes in you'll drown!"

Vi King: It served them right!

Odin: They were so terrified that they offered Suttung the mead of poetry if only he'd spare them. When they told him what brilliant stuff it was he agreed straight away and took their entire supply of mead back to Jotunheim.

Vi King: So, how did you get to hear about it?

Odin: Suttung was a born show-off and he began telling everyone about how *he* was the new owner of the mead of poetry. So I *soon* got news of it.

Vi King: And what did you do?

Odin: "Right!" I thought to myself, "We gods are having *that* back!" It's *ours* anyway – its main ingredient being Kvasir, who *we* made. So I disguised myself as a giant called Bolverk and made my way to Jotunheim where I spotted nine thralls working in a field.

49

Vi King: You mean peasants?

Odin: Yes. I asked one of them who his boss was and he told me it was Baugi.

Vi King: Suttung's brother!

Odin: I realized I'd struck lucky so I whipped out my sharpening stone and put a fine new edge on his scythe for him. A few seconds later his pals gathered around and asked if I'd sharpen their scythes too.

Vi King: Hmmph! Dumbos!

Odin: "Oh I can't be bothered," I said. "I'll chuck my stone into the air and whoever catches it can keep it!"

Vi King: I bet *that* caused chaos.

Odin: I'll say! You should have seen the halfwits scramble. They were pushing and shoving while their scythes were flashing this way and that. In less than two minutes the whole lot lay dead on the grass with their throats cut!

Vi King: Ha ha ha. Typical thralls!

Odin: Next, I made my way to Baugi's cottage and asked him for food. "You must be joking!" he spluttered. "I've just discovered that all my stupid thralls have slaughtered each other. And I've still got fields full of crops to harvest!"

Vi King: What a brilliant opportunity to get in with him!

Odin: It was! I told him I was as strong as an ox and he hired me on the spot. I got his crops in in no time!

Vi King: Was he pleased?

Odin: Not half! He said he'd give me anything I wanted.

Vi King: I bet I can guess what you asked for!

Odin: I said I'd like a sip of the mead that I'd heard his brother had got hidden away inside the Hnitborg mountain

Vi King: And did he agree?

Odin: He wasn't madly keen on the idea but he did go and ask his brother.

Vi King: And did he get you some mead?

Odin: Course not. Suttung told him to get lost. Baugi was frightened of him. And scared of me. So I decided to use this to my advantage.

Vi King: What did you do?

Odin: I told him that his brother was a skinflint and that we should help ourselves to the mead just to teach the big schmuck a lesson.

Vi King: Did he agree to *that*?

Odin: Yes, but his heart wasn't in it. He was very useful though because he used his magic drill to bore a tunnel through the mountainside. By the way – I'm not boring you am I?

Vi King: No no carry on! I'm enjoying every twist and turn of your story!

Odin: The moment he got through to the secret chamber where the mead was stored I transformed myself into a snake and slithered up the passage. Only just in time too! Baugi had taken his dagger out to stab me!

Vi King: What a creep!

Odin: After some nifty wiggling I came face to face with Suttung's beautiful daughter who was guarding the barrels of mead. "Hello there gorgeous!" I said. "Hi handsome!" she replied.

Vi King: What? She said *that* ... to a snake?

Odin: No, I'd turned myself back into a giant by this time. A good-looking one too! She told me she was called Gunnlod. "A pretty name for an even prettier girl!" I said.

Vi King: You big charmer!

Odin: I asked if there was any chance of a couple of sweet kisses. "All right then, potato face," she said.

"But only six or seven thousand, mind. I don't want you thinking I'm the sort of girl who falls in love with the first one-eyed ogre who comes along!" It was obvious she was nuts about me!

Vi King: I think I can see where this is leading.

Odin: After some serious snogging and whatnot she told me that she was mine for ever and would give me anything to prove her eternal love for me.

Vi King: And you said?

Odin: "How about a sip of the old fellah's mead of poetry then?"

Vi King: And she replied?

Odin: "Ooh, I don't know about that? My dad would go crazy if he found out!" "Oh go on. Just a sip?" I said, giving one of her enormous barrels a friendly squeeze. "All right then," she giggled. "But just a *tinsy, winsy, little sipsy wipsy*, mind!" "Of course my beloved," I said. And with that I picked up the mead barrels and drained *every last drop* from them!

Vi King: But – what about…?

Odin: Don't worry! I didn't *swallow* any of it. I just held it under my tongue.

Vi King: *Big* mouth!

Odin: Cheeky! Next I pulled my masterstroke and turned into an eagle. I flew down the passage and out into the light as fast as I could. I heard a huge roar behind me.

Vi King: What was that, then?

Odin: It was Gunnlod's dad, Suttung. He'd found out what was going on and had turned *himself* into an eagle too! And now he was after me!

Vi King: Did he catch you?

Odin: Almost! We swooped, we dived and we soared, and eventually we came within sight of Asgard. As I approached the city walls I could see lots of activity below me. The other gods must have seen me coming. They were scurrying around setting out pots and pans and barrels to receive the mead of poetry which was sloshing around in my mouth at that very moment.

Vi King: Ooh … this *is* exciting!

Odin: Just as I crossed the wall I felt one of Suttung's talons strike my wing tip. The shock caused me to spill a tiny drop of mead on the ground outside Asgard but I generally managed to keep my beak tight shut. As soon as I landed I spat all of the remaining liquid into the crocks and jars.

Vi King: Hurrah! Well done you! Wow – that really is some story, Odin!

Odin: Yes, Vi. That is how I rescued the mead of poetry. The magic elixir that was to give "poetry power" to generations to come. Now, when I wish to give an ordinary person the ability to weave spells with words I let them drink the mead. Look back through history and you will no doubt be able to identify many of the magicians of language who have drunk of this super-booze ... Shakespeare, Wordsworth, Keats and Roald Dahl to name but a few.

Vi King: But what about the dribble you spilled outside the walls of Asgard?

Odin: Oh, that drop wasn't worth worrying about. I left *that* for the composers of rugby songs, creators of advertising jingles and third-rate TV scripts, investigative reporters and such like – many of them certainly seem to need it.

Vi King: Any chance of a swig then?

Odin: Now Vi on earth would you want that?

FANTASTIC FACTS 3: ODIN

1 Top Norse god Odin was not only the god of poetry but also the god of battle and death. His was the sort of job that demanded knowledge of all things so one of the first things that young Odin did was to get himself thoroughly *"well"* educated. He did this by paying a visit to the Well of Mimir which lay next to the roots of Yggdrasil, the World Tree (see page 22). It was said that if you drank from this well you would instantaneously become clever and wise and knowledgeable beyond your wildest dreams. However, there was a price to pay for this instant education. Mimir, the guardian of the "fountain of wisdom", told Odin that in exchange for just one swig of the wacky water he must first pluck out an eye (his own, not Mimir's!) and bung it down the well. Odin, being a real swot, did exactly as he was told, drank the water and immediately became cleverer than a truckload of teachers.

In later life though, he got a bit self-conscious about his missing peeper and often wore a big floppy hat or a hood to hide the empty socket. Nevertheless his Viking worshippers were all really appreciative of the great sacrifice he'd made on their behalf and never forgot that he was up there in Asgard keeping an eye out for them.

2 Even after drinking from Mimir's Well, Odin still wasn't entirely satisfied that he knew absolutely *everything*. So some time later he decided to hang himself from Yggdrasil for nine whole days just to be entirely sure that there weren't any other vital bits of wisdom and knowledge that he'd missed out on. You probably won't be surprised to hear that this rather desperate method of self-improvement proved to be fatal. But fortunately, being a god, Odin was restored to life by magic and in his "born again" form he now possessed more wisdom than anyone in the world.

3 The other thing that Odin got from hanging around in the woods was the runes. This isn't a Scandinavian stomach upset brought on by spending too much time pinned to trees. It is actually a special sort of mystical writing which is said to have magic powers. When Odin

returned to the land of the living he was suddenly gifted with the miraculous ability to write stories, poems, magic spells (and really pretty notes for his milkman).

Most Vikings were so busy being the playground bullies of northern Europe that they didn't have time to get to grips with the runes, but a few incredibly swotty ones (Sven the Pen? Eric the Anorak?) did do the occasional bit of runic writing. They carved their runes on to wood, stone, metal and bone. They're mainly made up of straight lines because short sharp strokes are much easier to cut out than the swirls and flicks that us modern swots are all so fond of. They'd have to wait until newfangled pens and paper became available before they could do that kind of thing! The runes do contain a bit of information about the Norse gods and their world but they're so incredibly difficult to understand that even the brainiest of professors have a terrible time making head or tail of them. Runes accompanied by brightly coloured patterns are sometimes found on stones in Scandinavia. (*Tip:* If you are ever wandering around Sweden and come across a rune-stone with the inscription *Stockholm FC Rule OK* … treat it with caution!)

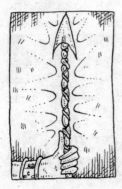 **4** Odin had an ace spear called Gungnir which was made from a branch of Yggdrasil and carved with magic runes. No matter how carelessly he threw this weapon it always found its intended target. (Either that or he fooled everyone into believing that he'd really been aiming for whatever Gungnir happened to hit.)

5 Odin sat on an enormous throne called Hlidskialf which was part watchtower and part comfy seat – a bit like those things that life guards and tennis umpires sit on, but rather grander and taller. From this lofty perch Odin could see almost everything that went on anywhere in the nine worlds.

6 Probably as a result of being well educated, Odin was a cunning and crafty sort of god. He once used his amazing cleverness to save his life when threatened by a clever giant called Vafthrudnir. Odin challenged the giant to an ancient Norse version of University Challenge. Whoever lost the contest would give his head to his opponent. Odin answered all the giant's questions successfully and the giant nearly managed to answer all of Odin's questions correctly but he got stuck on the last one. Odin had asked Vafthrudnir to repeat the words he'd whispered into his son Balder's ear. In view of the fact that Balder was dead at the time, Vafthrudnir hadn't the faintest idea what Odin had said to him so he had to admit defeat and give his head to Odin.

7 Occasionally Odin would disguise himself as a human and go for a wander around Midgard. During his days out he would sometimes meet a human woman he quite liked and then spend some time chatting to her and generally having fun. As a result of these romantic episodes quite a few Vikings actually believed that Odin was their dad.

8 As he was an all-powerful mega-god, Odin didn't actually ever need to eat any food at all but he was rather partial to the occasional goblet of mead. The only food he came into contact with were the huge chunks of meat which he fed to his two pet wolves, Geri and Freki. In return, Geri and Freki were said to bring him good luck (and his carpet slippers).

9 Unfortunately, Odin's vast knowledge and wisdom, particularly his premonitions about the end of the world, made him a rather unhappy sort of a god and in most portraits he appears to be rather sad, if not downright miserable – which is probably why he enjoyed the occasional drink of mead. In addition to being a misery guts, Odin could be quite spiteful and envious at times, even where his own children and grandchildren were concerned. When Thor once gave a horse to his own son Magni, rather

than to Odin, Odin became very jealous and decided to use his magic powers to get his revenge. Some time later, when Thor was trying to cross a swollen river, he met a ferryman called Harbard. Not only did Harbard refuse to ferry Thor across the water, but he also told him that his mum was dead and his wife had run off with a human! He then began to tease Thor and outdo his tales of bravery with even better ones of his own. This made Thor very angry indeed and it wasn't until he got back to Asgard that he realized that the ferryman had been telling him porkies and his mum was really OK and his wife was still at home. What he didn't realize though, was that Harbard was really Odin. He'd misused his magic to transform himself into a ferryman so he could wreak his childish revenge on his own son. And him a top god too! Pathetic really, isn't it?

10 Other warlike northern European peoples had gods who were their own versions of Odin and who were given names like Woden and Wotan. The day of the week which we now know as Wednesday (Odin's day or Woden's day) is named after him.

LEGEND 4: THOR'S SUPER-HAMMER GOES MISSING

Do you own something that's really, really special to you? Something that you think of as your most treasured possession and just wouldn't dream of ever parting company with? It could be something as simple as a battered old pair of trainers that you've had for ages ... or as cool (and useful!) as a mountain bike or new super-computer. Have you ever wondered how you'd feel if this most treasured possession suddenly disappeared? You'd probably feel just like the missing item, i.e. absolutely *lost*! ... maybe even devastated! Number four of our ten best ever is the legend that tells how the Norse god, Thor, lost a great treasure, and the adventures and scrapes he got himself into trying to get it back. And it was absolutely *essential* for him to retrieve it – if he didn't, the entire world would be beset by all kinds of dreadful problems ... including a rather unpleasant and inconvenient everlasting winter! Although this is a legend that's thousands of years old we've brought it up to date a bit. Those Vikings may have been a bloodthirsty lot – but in many ways they were quite similar to people living in the early twenty-first century … and they definitely had a sense of humour!

One morning Thor, the great Norse God of thunder, fighting and general all round thuggishness, awoke to find that something very dear to him had disappeared from under his very nose.

"Oh no!!" cried Thor, leaping from his bed, "Someone's only gone and nicked me bloomin' 'ammer!"

He immediately began rampaging around his house in a frantic search for the missing hammer. After demolishing several walls, ripping apart every scatter cushion he could lay his enormous hairy hands on *and* reducing his Scandinavian pine kitchen units to matchwood with his bare teeth, he still couldn't find his beloved hammer. (As you may well have guessed by now, cool, calm logical thinking and painstaking searches weren't Thor's strong points.)

Ignoring the pathetic bleats of his beloved goats, Toothgnasher and Toothgrinder, Thor picked up their breakfast barrel, emptied it into his cavernous mouth, swallowed the lot, belched thunderously, then stormed out into the garden for a good sulk. At that moment, Loki, the god of mischief, happened to pass by.

"Mornin' Thor, me old mate!" he said, as he watched Thor fling his best war chariot into the next door neighbour's fishpond, "Got the miseries 'ave we ... or are you just 'avin' a bit of a tidy up?"

"No ... I've gone and lost me blitherin' 'ammer," Thor mumbled into his huge red beard.

"Oooh, there's no need to get your magic belt in a twist over *that*!" laughed Loki. "I'm forever losing tools and things. Just go and buy yourself a new one!"

"Listen, Loki!" thundered Thor (as only *he* knew how). "I'm not talking hammers for puttin' up shelves ... or even hammers for knockin' sense into gods of mischief! I'm talkin' hammers made from meteorites by mysterious dwarves deep in the bowels of the earth. You know, *magic* hammers for beating the living daylights out of monsters and giants, and hurling half-way across the world and saving whole kingdoms from evil enemies – not to mention the ravages of ice and frost and snow!" He paused for a moment then proudly added, "As only I know how!!"

Loki went pale. "You don't mean ... you don't think that someone's *stolen* Mjollnir, your *super-hammer*, do you!?" he whispered anxiously.

"Yes," said Thor, "Exactly!"

After he'd taken in the terrible news of the loss of Thor's magic hammer, Loki thought for a while, then he said, "Well, you know who'll have nicked it, don't you? It'll be one of those pesky frost giants from that cursed frozen land of Jotunheim. Those big bullies would nick the breath from their own grannies if you gave them half the chance!"

A glimmer of understanding caused Thor's huge, red eyebrows to quiver with excitement. "*Of course*, it would be them!" he exclaimed, "Why didn't *I* think of that?"

"Because you're as thick as two planks!" Loki explained helpfully.

"*What* did you say?!" rumbled Thor.

"I said, 'I think it's one of their pranks'," said Loki.

"I think you're right." agreed Thor.

"Well," said Loki, "I'll tell you what I'll do, Thor. As I haven't got much on today, I'll just turn meself into a bird and have a flutter over the giants' land and see what I can find out."

"Ooh, ta ever so, Loki," said Thor gratefully.

"OK. Must fly – see ya later, giant-hater!" said Loki, and went off to turn himself into a bird.

"Sometimes that Loki's a real treasure!" said Thor to himself.

Loki was back in what seemed like no time at all. Thor stopped twiddling his beard and looked curiously at the little bird that had just landed at his feet.

"I was right!" chirruped the bird, hopping excitedly from one foot to the other.

"Stone the crows – a talkin' bird!" gasped Thor.

"No, it's not a talkin' bird, you great big bonehead – it's me, Loki!" squeaked the bird, "Hang on a mo' – I'll just turn meself back into a god!" In a flurry of feathers and shower of breadcrumbs, Loki was his old god-like self again. "I was right," he continued, "Thrym, the giant King of Jotunheim has stolen your hammer and he says he won't give it back unless Freyja agrees to marry him."

This wasn't in the least bit surprising to either Thor or Loki. Thrym the Giant had fancied Freyja for absolutely ages – and after all, she was the Norse goddess of love *and* mind bogglingly beautiful! The two gods immediately rushed round to her house to ask her if she fancied marrying Thrym.

"You must be joking!" said Freyja. "I wouldn't marry that overgrown apology for an ogre for all the reindeer cutlets in Asgard. He's got a face like a warthog's widdler and all the sex appeal of a sack full of recently strangled ferrets … and more to the point … I'm already married! So bog off, both of you!"

And with that she caught Loki with a powerful left hook that sent him and Thor tumbling through the doorway of her palace.

"Charming behaviour for the goddess of love … *I'm* sure!" said Loki as he picked bits of broken teeth out of Freyja's front door mat.

"No spirit of of adventure … that's her trouble!" said Thor.

"There's only one thing for it, Thor, me old mate!" said Loki, "*You'll* just have to pretend to be Freyja!"

"What!" said Thor, turning as pink as a Scandinavian sunset, "I can't do that! I haven't got any … err, you know…"

"Ruby red lips?" suggested Loki.

"Exactly!" said Thor. "Or any…"

"Golden curls?"

"Them as well!"

"No problem, big buddy," said Loki, "We'll give you an all-over makeover! You'd be amazed at the tricks they get up to nowadays with lip-sticks, pan-sticks and ready-mix! And in the meantime we'll let Thrym know that we agree to the terms of his ransome. Your … sorry … *Freyja's*, hand in marriage for the return of Mjollnir."

One hour later, Thor – one of the toughest, roughest, all fighting, all action, no nonsense Norse gods ever – was looking absolutely stunning in a tartan mini skirt, skin-tight taffeta tank-top and stiletto heeled, seal-skin, sling-backs.

"I feel like a right big elf's blouse, I do," Thor grumbled to Loki as he caught sight of his fox-fur false eyelashes in the mirror. "Do I *have* to do this?"

"Remember little Mjollnir!' said Loki.

"Ay, less of the little!" muttered Thor, "That's no ordinary hammer you're talking about!"

Later that same afternoon the two gods were making their way up the steep mountain track that led to Thrym's massive black castle and Thor was casting furtive glances at Loki's purple velvet maxi dress and rat-skin ankle boots.

"I don't feel half so silly now you're wearing that soppy maidservant's outfit," he whispered, as they approached the oak door of the giant's stronghold.

"A brilliant finishing touch you must agree, Thor ... er I mean ... *Madam*!" squeaked Loki from beneath his lamb's wool shawl. Then he added in a whisper, "Now listen, Thunderguts! When we get to Thrym's place don't forget to act like a love goddess and not like a polar bear in a penguin pond ... OK?"

"OK," muttered Thor, somewhat sulkily.

At that moment the huge castle door opened to reveal Thrym himself. It was obvious that the giant king was completely nuts about Freyja. As soon as he set eyes on his bride-to-be he blushed a deep shade of pink and began blowing her kisses from the tips of his fencepost-sized fingers.

"Oh no!" muttered Thor, "Just look at him! What in Asgard have I gone and got myself into?"

"He's barmy about you!" whispered Loki. "Look, you can see the stars in his eyes! Hmmm ... I wonder if he's a good snogger?"

By the time they reached him, Thrym had completely overcome his shyness and without a moment's hesitation he threw his arms around Thor and smothered him in wet, slobbery kisses.

"Oh my god!" groaned Thor, twisting and turning in an attempt to escape the giant's passionate embrace.

"Oh my ... *goddess*!" gasped Thrym, holding Thor at arms length so he could admire the radiant beauty of the love of his life! "Welcome, Freyja, my little passion flower," he crooned. "Greetings my fragrant little honey

69

bunch. Follow me … the wedding feast awaits!"

Thrym led Thor and Loki into a vast hall that was absolutely packed to the rafters with laughing, feasting giants. As they entered they were greeted by enthusiastic cheering and several shouts of "Wow, what a cracker!" and "It's not fair, Thrym gets all the best birds!"

"Shall we begin my dear?" said Thrym, as soon as they were seated "I suppose you're feeling quite peckish after your journey?"

"Not half!" squeaked Thor "I'm absolutely *starving!*"

One whole roast ox and eight grilled salmon later Thor downed the last of his third barrelful of mead, wiped his lips on the back of his sleeve, patted his stomach, then let rip with a botty belch so loud and earth-shattering it actually made some of the older giants think the hall was being invaded by a whale which had recently swallowed a boat load of baked beans. They all stopped eating and looked in amazement at the "goddess of love" – who was now contentedly picking her teeth with an enormous hunting knife.

It was obvious that the giants were beginning to have their doubts about this beautiful "woman" … especially Thrym! Loki noticed that the giant king had been looking at Thor rather curiously for some time and he decided that some sort of distraction (preferably followed by some drastic action) was needed, so he quickly said, "Excuse me your Hugeness, don't you think that this is the appropriate moment to present the wedding gift?"

"Yes, yes ... why not?" agreed Thrym absentmindedly, and waved over a couple of servants who'd been waiting in a corner of the great hall.

Thor's eyes lit up when he saw that they were carrying his beloved Mjollnir. "And now my dear," said Thrym, taking Mjollnir from the servants and presenting it to Thor. "Here is my wedding gift to you and all your family."

"Right! Let him have it!" yelled Loki. "It's now or never!"

"But I am letting him have—" Thrym began to say but he never managed to finish his sentence because Thor leapt up from the table, snatched Mjollnir from his hands and floored him with a devastating blow to his enormous head.

The next few minutes were a blur of action in which Thor, high heels, mini skirt and all, raced around the hall toppling giants like skyscrapers in an earthquake. They didn't stand a chance! Loki did think about joining in the fun but by the time he'd picked up a giant-sized serving spoon to dish out a bit of grief of his own there wasn't much left for him to do. Thor and his formidable superhammer, Mjollnir, had struck again and again and the hall was strewn with dozens of moaning, groaning giants.

"Well!" said Loki, as he and Thor staggered triumphantly out of Thrym's castle. "That'll certainly make them think twice next time they're planning to pinch other folks' magic weapons!"

Thor didn't seem to hear him as he was busy looking down at his feet.

"Oh, just look at *that*!" he said impatiently. "Would you *believe* it!?"

"Would I believe *what*?" said Loki, suddenly alarmed.

"That!" cried Thor irritably, pointing to his feet. "I've only gone and snapped one of the straps on me best pair of sling-backs!"

FANTASTIC FACTS 4: THOR

1 His status Thor was one of the top three Norse gods. The rough, tough Viking warriors and seafarers absolutely worshipped him because he was a god after their own heart, i.e. the sort of god who bashed first and asked questions afterwards (but only if he could manage to think of any!). Many of the legends about Thor describe him making short work of the sort of things that made everyday life very, very difficult for the average Viking … things like huge wolves, enormous hostile seas and icebergs the size of Mexico (caused by the

frost giants of course) – not to mention axe-wielding barbarians!

HOW WOULD THOR DEAL WITH THIS?

As a mark of their respect and awe for the heroic and all-powerful Thor, many Vikings gave themselves and their children names like Thorsteinn and Thorfinnr (if they were boys) and Thorgerdr and Thorgunnr (if they were girls) – in rather the same way as some people now name their children after sports heroes and movie stars.

2 His family background Thor belonged to the family of gods called the Aesir who, as you know, were generally the sort of gods you probably wouldn't want to live next-door to. His dad, Odin, was king of all the gods, but even he wasn't half so warlike as his rootin' tootin', up-and-at-'em son. His mum was Jord. Both Odin and Jord recognized their bouncing bundle of joy's potential for a life of action and heroics when, moments after he was born, he began playfully tossing huge stacks of bearskins about as if they weighed no more than a feather (rather than just sucking his thumb and being sick all over his baby grow).

Thor's first wife was the giantess, Iarnsaxa, with whom he had a couple of children called Magni and Modi. He later married the beautiful goddess Sif and they had a daughter called Thrud who was built like a giantess but was also as gorgeous as a goddess. Thrud was fancied (and looked up to) by lots of chaps including a remarkably clever dwarf called Alvis.

74

3 His hammer Thor's favourite toy was Mjollnir, his hammer. The name means the Destroyer. It was made by two dwarves and was so powerful it could flatten a mountain in one go. Thor could actually throw this hammer halfway across the world and it would always hit its target! And what's more, he wouldn't even have to go and ask for his deadly weapon back – its magic powers made sure it found its own way back to his hand.

4 His worst enemies Thor couldn't abide the frost giants and he loathed monsters (they weren't too mad about him either). He was forever having mass scraps with them and bashing their brains in with good old Mjollnir.

The Viking legends are full of gruesome tales of Thor and his mighty hammer. Such is his fame for acts of courage and daring that during the twentieth century Thor has even been made the star of a "Marvel" comic strip.

5 His important peacetime jobs Thor used Mjollnir to chip away the ice and snow at the end of the harsh Scandinavian winter so that the rivers would flow and the flowers would grow. People who had to endure the incredibly cold winters of northern Europe obviously found it very comforting to know that good old Thor and his ice-breaking hammer would come along every year and save them all from permanent petrification – during the spring thaw.

As well as being responsible for making sure that the atrocious Scandinavian weather didn't get completely out of hand, Thor's other important task was to ensure that crops flourished during the growing season and provide the Norse people with enough grain to see them through their bleak winter.

6 His incredibly useful fashion accessories Thor had a really brilliant belt which doubled his strength when he wore it. This was perfect for dealing with playground bullies (and also quite useful for holding his trousers up). In addition, he had a pair of iron gloves which he had to wear if he wanted his magic hammer to do its stuff – this must have made battles on hot summer afternoons really uncomfortable.

7 How he got about Thor dashed around in a chariot pulled by two gigantic goats called Toothgnasher and Toothgrinder. (If anything got in their way they would just give a few short blasts on their horns.) Even when he wasn't using his chariot Thor could move very swiftly indeed as his feet were made from thunderbolts, which came in incredibly useful whenever he was in need of a bit of nifty legwork.

8 His thunder Thor was the only god who wasn't allowed to leave Asgard via Bifrost, the rainbow bridge. This was because it was feared that his thunderous footsteps or those of his goats would cause serious structural damage to the bridge (resulting in massive rush-hour tail-backs). Thor was therefore made to go the long way round which meant crossing the legendary rivers of Ormt and Kormt.

9 His mighty mouth Thor's voice was supposed to be so loud and powerful and scary that he could shout during a pitched battle and everyone would be able to hear him despite the awful screams and shouts and clash of weapons. In fact his voice was said to be so frightening that his enemies were supposed to drop down in a dead faint when they heard it. (In other words he had a voice just like a *teacher's*!)

As well as using his mighty mouth to yell people into submission, Thor was also fond of filling it (and his stomach) with vast quantities of food. His appetite was enormous and sometimes he would consume several roast oxen at one go (and that was just for starters!).

10 How we remember him One of our days of the week is named after Thor – bet you can't guess which one. Yes, that's it – Monday … ha ha … only joking! But seriously, have you noticed how on a Thor's day your teachers are all just that bit more ferocious and less patient – perhaps they're all descended from Vikings?

LEGEND 5: GOODIES FOR THE GODDIES

Our fifth legend is a tale of mischief and magic. The stars of this legend are the little folk who lived under Midgard. The ancient Norse knew that there were lots of precious and useful metals and gemstones buried under the ground and they also knew that some people had special skills and talents for turning these raw materials into very useful and beautiful objects. In the Viking legends it was the dwarves who were said to possess these abilities and they spent their days creating lots of fab goodies for the gods. These industrious and inventive little chaps were obviously the ancient Norse equivalent of the modern day technological whizz kids who spend *their* lives buried away (in factories and laboratories) dreaming up the amazing gizmos and gadgets that are intended to make our lives more convenient and exciting.

Of course, the world of the Viking legends is the sort of place where *anything* can happen so the dwarves were able to add a generous dash of magic to the things they made. As a result their gifts for the gods were very, very special indeed and make even the most high-tech modern stuff look dull by comparison!

Just as there is competition between modern manufacturers to see who can come up with the best designs, there was also great rivalry between the dwarves. Legend 5 is told through an extract from the diary of just such an ambitious, competitive and jealous dwarf…

A DAY IN THE LIFE OF A BUSINESS DWARF, by DVALIN, vertically challenged crafts-person, goldspinner and elfxecutive-director of… 'GOODS FOR THE GODS - GOOD GOD THEY'RE GOOD!' trading as DWARFTECH plc (tm) Head Office: Diligence Cavern, Enterprise Trading Grotto, Svartlheim The Netherworld.

Runesday - 45th Moon'swain   ME

10.00 Loki the Trickster came to see me. He was in trouble (yes, again!) While Thor's Wife, Sif was having forty winks, he'd sneaked into her sleeping chamber and cut off all that lovely, long blonde hair of hers and left it strewn around the floor. Said he did it for a laugh! Strange sense of humour, if you ask me! When Sif awoke to find she'd lost her famous golden tresses she was absolutely horrified. Also somewhat distressed (ha-ha!) And Thor didn't see the funny side of things when he discovered that his "fair-headed" wife had become his "bare-headed" wife. He soon found out who the phantom hairdresser was and offered him the face transplant he'd never wanted. Loki quickly said he knew of a little tress-maker and promised he'd have Sif a new top knot in a jiffy.

So that's why Loki turned up here. Not only did he want us to spin Sif a brand new head of hair from the finest gold but he also wanted us to weave some of our magic into it so it would grow just like the normal stuff. Plus he asked us if we'd throw in a couple of extra special gifts for the other gods. They were none too pleased with his antics and he needed to get back in their good books.

At first I wasn't too happy about any of this but it occured to me that it might be good for business. I decided to look upon it as a sort of prestige "giftware for gods" promotion that might bring in some big orders from Asgard. So we got busy straight away!

11:00 Fabulous blonde wig for Sif was ready. Us dwarves don't mess about! World famous for teamwork and productivity!

11·15 Special gift for Odin ready. Snazzy new spear knocked up by one of our top creative whizz kids. Definitely at the cutting edge of weapon technology. Got magical target seeking device. <u>NEVER</u> misses! Also completely unbreakable. Decided to call it Gungnir.

11·30 Special gift for Freyr ready. Superb new sailing ship conjured up by our maritime engineering boffin. Named it Skinbladnir. Magnificent fully rigged vessel with fab figurehead, golden anchors and seasoned oak hull. All completely foldaway. Activate a couple of spring clips and the whole thing closes to handkerchief size. Slips easily into owners' pocket or wallet. Convenient... ...or what! Who said dwarves are only good for hanging around in underpasses? World leaders in quality product innovation more like!

11·40 Loki set off for Asgard carrying the goodies. I decided to follow him. Just to make sure that Brokk and Eitri, those conniving rivals of ours down the tunnel, didn't get to see OUR exciting and EXCLUSIVE new designs. I shadowed him through the maze of subways and underpasses that lead back to the upper world. Could see he was dying to play with the merchandise!

11:55 Loki reached the cavern with underground lake and STOPPED! Right outside **MICRO-DWARF** plc. Yes! Brokk and Eitri's HQ! (Oh no!) Trickster put on Sif's golden hair-piece. Took a butcher's at the reflection in the water. Let out a wolf whistle! Next he took Gungnir from sheath. Aimed at tiny pebble fifty metres away. Closed eyes and threw. Bang on target! Spear undamaged. Finally, he slipped Skinbladnir out of carrying pouch. Released natty little catches. Next moment, fifty metre super-ship was floating across lake. Magic!

12:00 I got a terrible shock! Noticed that door to **MICRO-DWARF** plc was open! Saw two pairs of eyes glittering in darkness. Yes! Brokk and Eitri had been watching the whole time. And seen OUR new products!

12·05 Brokk and Eitri came out of **MICRO-DWARF**. Sidled over to Loki. Asked him if he'd been shopping, where he'd got the "cheapo trash"! (I nearly burst a blood vessel!) Loki pointed in direction of MY workshop. Heard Brokk laugh and say something about "Dwarfitat!" Then heard Eitri describe MY products "elf-assembly rubbish"! and say that they could do loads better! I was furious (nearly wet myself!) Some sort of dispute then broke out between the brothers.

12·10 All three STILL arguing. Loki saying that he bet they couldn't make better products and them saying that they could. Finally, Loki yelled, "I bet you MY HEAD you can't!" and Brokk and Eitri told him he was on. All three rushed into **MICRO-DWARF** HQ..... but FORGOT to lock the door!

12·15 Made sure coast was clear, then crept into premises of **MICRO-DWARF** (perfect opportunity for industrial espionage, ooh, ooh!). Positioned myself behind extra fat stalactite. Pencil and notebook at the ready!

12·20 Brothers made Loki at home in their hospitality area. Comfy chair, horn of mead, that sort of thing. Then went off to workshop. I followed!

13·30 Much tapping, puffing and blowing in metal-working area. After which, Eitri pulled golden arm bracelet from magic furnace. He cooled it in water-trough, then set it to one side.

14·00 More hammering, clanging, wheezing of bellows and roaring from furnace. Magnificent newly-forged hammer suddenly appeared on Brokk's anvil. As if by magic! What am I talking about? It was by MAGIC! what else?

14·55 Eitri took down whole pigskin from the workshop wall. Due to room being full of steam, smoke and sparks I couldn't quite make out the exact technical details of the next operation. But the results were awesome!

15·10 Lots of coughs and splutters from Eitri. Followed by snorts and squeals! Smoke and steam suddenly cleared. Enormous golden wild boar now standing in middle of workshop! Wow! (Even though I do say it myself.)

15·25 Eitri entered hospitality area with the golden ring. Slipped it on Loki's arm, muttered some sort of magic incantation and tapped it three times. Eight more rings appeared, all perfect copies of the first! Eitri then told Loki that the ring was called Draupnir and would reproduce itself like that every ninth night for ever more. Loki obviously very impressed. [Me too!]

15·40 Brokk led mega-boar into hospitality area and told Loki it was called Gullinbursti. Eitri then extinguished the flaming torches that lit the cave. But whole place was <u>STILL</u> bathed in a brilliant light! All coming from the <u>PIG</u>! Light sensitive bristles of course! Each one probably at least 1000 imp output. Perfect for endless Norse nights! Now, why didn't <u>WE</u> think of that!

15·45 Eitri pointed out power-porker's other ace features to Loki. Four trotter drive, massive fuel economy, lean burn appetite and advanced gruel injection! No terrain too difficult.... swamps, glaciers, impassable mountain passes! A real driver's pig if ever there was one!

Made note to get on to own research and development dwarves working on rival vehicle. Maybe call it, err....Rover?

16·00 Eitri presented the magnificent hammer to Loki. Details as follows.

Name:- Mjollnir.

Description:- Enemy seeking inter-worlds war hammer

Method of use:- Choose target, anywhere, distance no object! Sling

Result:- Enemy destroyed. Hammer automatically returns to thrower after impact!

16·30 Loki left **MICRO-DWARF** with gifts accompanied by Brokk. I followed.

18·00 Loki arrived back in Asgard. Odin chuffed to bits with new spear and arm ring. Thor over the moon with Mjollnir. Said he couldn't wait to splatter a giant! Freyr said Skinbladnir was just sort of ship he'd always wanted and Gullinbursti would be great for chariot pulling. Sniff... sorry <u>Sif</u>, so pleased with golden hairdo she actually stopped blubbering. **18·20** Sort of god's focus group was organized by Loki. He asked them to choose best gift of the lot. No contest. Mjollnir voted outright winner. Perfect anti-giant defence weapon for gods!

18·25 So Brokk got his result! Grinned from one pointy ear to other and took out knife ready to cut off his prize. i.e. Loki's head - as agreed in bet!

18·26 Loki looked alarmed, then suddenly brightened up. Told Brokk he could have his head **BUT** mustn't damage neck whilst cutting as **THAT** wasn't in the deal. Which of course, was impossible for Brokk! Brokk completely stumped. Knew he was beaten. Determined to have some sort of revenge though. Whipped out needle and thread and sewed up Loki's gob. Then scuttled off to Svartleheim laughing his socks off.

18·30 Watched Loki rip stitches out of mouth. You can't keep a bad god down or sew it seams! (ha ha)

18·45 I arrived back at **DWARFTECH.** **COMPLETELY** stressed out. What a day! Memo to self: Call urgent board meeting to discuss serious market challenge from **MICRO-DWARF.** Looks like they're ahead of the game!

FANTASTIC FACTS 5: THE LITTLE FOLK

1 How they arrived When Odin and his brothers were busy making the world from Ymir's rapidly decomposing flesh they noticed that it was beginning to crawl with foul, wriggling things like maggots and other revoltingly squirmy objects far too horrible to mention. Rather than doing something entirely boring like squashing these repulsive little creatures between two large stones or using them as fishing bait they decided to turn them into dwarves and elves.

2 Where they live When the gods had finished making the dwarves (who were sometimes known as dark elves) they decided that they were far too ugly to be seen by ordinary folk so they insisted that they stay underground and keep themselves busy creating beautiful and useful gadgets for the convenience and enjoyment of their superiors, i.e. them, the gods. As the dwarves scrabbled around in the earth (Ymir's ex-flesh) they found all sorts of precious metals and gems. They quickly mastered the art of turning these raw materials into attractive knick-knacks and horrendously lethal weapons. They soon became master craftsmen and guarded the secrets of their trade most jealously. The dwarves' worlds were called Nidavellir and Svartalfheim and were far below the surface of Midgard.

3 How the Gods keep them there! In order to ensure that the dwarves didn't sneak out for a quick wander around Midgard and Asgard during daylight hours and give some unsuspecting god or human person a severe fright with their hideously ugly mushes, the gods decided to make them sunlight sensitive. Just one sunbeam touching their skin instantly turned them to stone. If you walk around the countryside in Scandinavia today you will notice many stones and rocks lying around all over the place. Believe it or not, these completely natural-looking objects haven't always been there! Many of them are actually petrified dwarves who nipped upstairs for a look at the world above ground but forgot to keep their eye on the time ... then ended up getting completely stoned.

4 The light elves The light elves were quite different from the dwarves in many ways. They were created from the more good natured and slightly less repulsive creepy crawlies and for their convenience they were allowed to live in the world of Alfheim which was much nearer to Midgard and Asgard. The elves did things like looking after flowers, flitting around the forest, entertaining birds and generally living a much elfier sort of life altogether. They were also big (small) mates with the fairies.

5 Their reputation Despite the fact that the elves came from slightly better-class backgrounds and were generally thought to be more good natured than the dwarves, the Vikings were quite frightened of them. This was because of their reputation for luring impressionable Norse teenagers off to the woods and getting them to do wild and crazy things like dancing in circles or hanging around fairy rings on moonlit nights. It was said that these teenagers were often never seen again because as soon as the first cock crowed at dawn the elves would spirit them back to Alfheim. (**Tip:** If you're ever in the woods at night and come across a group of elves who ask you if you fancy a bop or try to sell you some spotted toadstools just say "NO!", and then report them to your local neighbourhood watch ... or even your local neighbourhood witch!)

6 Trolls, gnomes and kobolds There were several other varieties of little people wandering around the world of the Viking legends including trolls, gnomes and kobolds. The kobolds were a type of dwarf who lived near to the houses of some Vikings and occasionally helped with their more difficult jobs like chopping firewood, moving bales of hay and defrosting the well. They were never actually seen by the Vikings because they performed all their helpful tasks under cover of darkness. Even today in modern Scandinavia some people still leave scraps of food and drinks out for the kobolds as they really do believe in the existence these "little folk". Other people actually think that the treasure of the dwarves still lies buried deep and occasionally attempt to find it – just as some people in Britain occasionally go looking for the Loch Ness monster. (In other words, they're completely barmy!)

7 Alvis One of the best known dwarves in the Norse myths was Alvis. He was the little chap who made many of the brilliant weapons that the gods found so incredibly useful in their battles with evil giants and monsters. As a reward for all his hard work the gods promised him that he could marry

Thor's daughter, Thrud. Thor wasn't a bit keen on the idea of his child getting hitched to a titch so

he asked Alvis to pop up to Asgard for a bit of a chat, saying that he wanted him to prove that he made up in brains what he lacked in centimetres. Crafty Thor then kept Alvis up all night asking him long and complicated questions. As day broke they were still at it, and Alvis had no choice but to go and join the stones.

8 Dvalin Dvalin was another dwarf who was turned to stone by the sun. After this unfortunate occurrence all the other dwarves rather unkindly began referring to the sun as Dvalin's Delight (which it obviously wasn't!). Despite the fact that the other dwarves took great pleasure in this 'ironic' joke about their friend's misfortune, Dvalin remained stoney faced about the whole matter.

9 Otter Otter was a dwarf who occasionally liked to wander around in the form of an otter! One day Loki spotted him in his otter shape and killed him. Otter's dad was furious and took Odin, Loki and Thor

prisoner, saying he would only release them on payment of a huge ransom.

10 Andvari Andvari was the king of the dwarves and he owned a horde of treasure. After Loki had killed Otter he took Andvari's treasure to pay the ransome. Andvari was so annoyed about this that he put a bad luck curse on the treasure and from that day on it brought misfortune to whoever owned it.

LEGEND 6:
THOR'S BIG FIGHT!

The ancient Norse were forever having to prove that they were up to dealing with the little frustrations that each day brings to all of us. You know the sort of things, don't you? Wild animals who see you as nothing more than a tasty mid-morning snack ... rival warriors whose idea of having a really good time is to tie you to a tree then remove all of your body parts very, very slowly ... and temperatures so low that your ears freeze completely solid then fall off the moment someone speaks to you!

What they needed were role models to inspire them and set them an example of how to deal with their daily difficulties. The number one role models for the Viking warriors were gods like Thor and Odin and the way they dealt with their enemies. Then they might remember our sixth legend, the story of Thor and Hrungnir, and feel all inspired and think "That's way do it!" (...but *still* get completely marmalised?).

This legend is a packed with rootin', tootin', up-an'-at-'em two-fisted action, so what better way to tell it than in the form of a modern adventure comic strip!

MIDWAY THROUGH THE BANQUET THOR RETURNED FROM A TRIP AND WAS AMAZED TO SEE A DRUNKEN GIANT SITTING AMONG THE GODS NOT ONLY EATING THEIR FOOD AND DRINKING OUT OF HIS OWN GOBLET BUT INSULTING THEM ALL AS WELL! HE WAS FURIOUS!!

WHAT'S HE DOING HERE? LET ME AT HIM.... I'LL SPLATTER HIM!!

CAN'T TOUCH ME — I'M A SPECIAL GUESHT...SHO THERE!

HE'S RIGHT THOR!

99

101

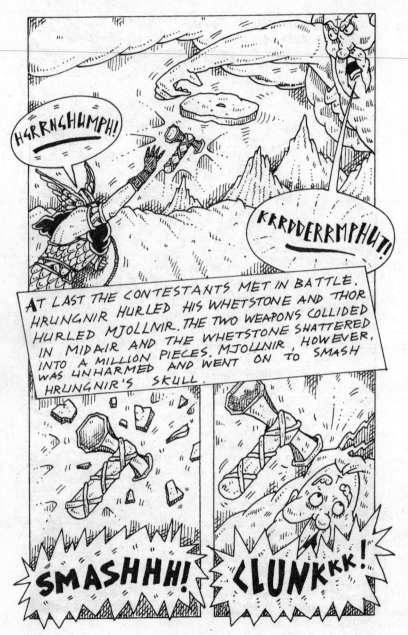

AS A REWARD FOR SAVING THE DAY THOR PRESENTED HIS TREMENDOUSLY TOUGH TODDLER WITH HRUNGNIR'S HORSE.

SO THAT'S IT THEN DADDY... YOUR'E FWEE. OOO!... AND I'M FWEE TOO... TEE HEE!

I'M RIGHT PROUD OF YOU, MAGNI LAD. HERE YOU CAN HAVE HRUNGNIR'S HORSE!

I WOULD HAVE PWEFERRED A THUNDER TUBBY!

EPILOGUE

THOR NEVER DID GET RID OF THAT FRAGMENT OF STONE FROM HIS FOREHEAD. WHILE HE WAS HAVING IT MAGICKED AWAY BY A SORCERESS HE BEGAN TELLING HER OF ONE OF HIS ADVENTURES WHICH INVOLVED HER HUSBAND. SHE BECAME SO INTERESTED IN THE STORY SHE QUITE FORGOT WHAT SHE WAS SUPPOSED TO BE DOING... SO HE ENDED UP KEEPING THE SOUVENIR OF HIS BIG FIGHT FOR THE REST OF HIS LIFE! BY THE WAY, WHEN YOU'RE OUT AND ABOUT WATCH OUT FOR BITS OF HRUNGNIR'S CLUB THAT ARE STILL LYING ON THE GROUND — THEY'RE THE STONE FRAGMENTS THAT WE NOW KNOW AS FLINTS.

FANTASTIC FACTS 6: EVERYTHING YOU'VE BEEN DYING TO KNOW ABOUT VALHALLA AND THE VALKYRIES (BUT WERE ALWAYS TOO CHICKEN TO ASK!)

Being brave and displaying limitless courage in the face of overwhelming danger was incredibly important to all of the ancient Norsemen. The greatest ambition of all self-respecting Viking warriors was to die a young and valiant death on the battlefield and then be whisked off to the great ex-serviceman's home in the sky known as Valhalla – preferably by one of its glamorous flying hostesses ... the Valkyries!

1 What was Valhalla? Valhalla was the hall where warriors slain in battle were taken. They were known as the Einherjar (the heroic dead). Odin was said to have created Valhalla as a sort of insurance policy in readiness for Ragnarok, the huge battle that was expected to take place some time around the end of the world. As he wasn't entirely sure of the *exact* date that this terrible event was scheduled for, he decided to stock-pile lots of brave dead warriors (and some "dead brave" ones) so that he'd at least be well prepared for it.

I TRUST YOU'RE ALL DEAD KEEN TO GO INTO BATTLE!

2 What was Valhalla like? The roofs of Valhalla were made from warriors' shields and its walls were built from hundreds of shining spears (which made wallpapering extremely tricky). The whole place was really ginormous and next to it a modern shopping mall would look really titchy. For example, every one of its *five hundred* doors was wide enough for the warriors to march through *eight hundred* abreast! (And if you think that's amazing you should have seen the size of the coconut doormats!) The idea of the big doors was to allow all the warriors to rush out on to the battlefield in a huge gang rather than having them queue up for hours on end and lose their mood for a scrap.

3 How did you get there? The slain warriors didn't make their own way to Valhalla because being dead made this a bit difficult for them. Instead they were taken there by beautiful maidens known as Valkyries who hung about in the sky just above battlefields watching out for particularly brave warriors who just happened to be in the process of dying valiantly and painfully. When they spotted a likely-looking candidate, the Valkyries would swoop down on their flying horses, then snatch him up and nip him back to Valhalla before he could as much as say "I think this severed head is going to profoundly

affect my chances of further success in this conflict"!
And then … they would make him better!

4 What sort of reception would you get? As a mark
of his respect for their courage Odin himself personally
welcomed the bravest warriors at the gates of Valhalla.
He would congratulate them on their brave deeds then
perhaps shake them warmly by the hand (or whatever
other bit of their anatomy they happened to have left).

5 What were the Valkyries like? The Valkyries were
very beautiful and charming but could also be extremely
cruel, particularly if they hung about battlefields too
long and got caught up in the excitement of the
occasion. Every now and again they would go
completely over the top and do something really
tasteless like pouring torrents of blood on the fighting
masses below them. Once they were even said to
have got so carried away that they began weaving
human intestines into an enormous tapestry and used

decapitated heads for the weights on their hastily improvised loom.

6 Is it possible to see a Valkyrie nowadays? Yes, in a way it is. The nineteenth century German composer Richard Wagner was absolutely nuts about the Norse gods and their various adventures and he wrote lots of operas about them. Some of them feature Valkyries and one of his most stirring bits of music is a piece called "The Ride Of the Valkyries". If you ever go to see a Wagner opera you will find it quite easy to recognize the Valkyries because they always wear large metal bras (a very sensible precaution considering the hazardous nature of their work).

7 How did the Valkyries get around? The Valkyries sometimes rode on wolves, but their preferred method of transport was to ride the beautiful horses who occasionally sprayed frost or water on to the earth below them as they galloped across the heavens. You can still see these magnificent mounts cantering across the sky today. People who lack an imagination or a sense of adventure and romance will insist on telling you that these great white steeds are now more accurately referred to as "clouds" (as if!).

8 Was there much to do up there? Once they were brought back to life, the slain warriors had an absolutely ace time. After a daily training session during which they knocked each other senseless and were then quickly mended by the Valkyries, they would return to the hall and spend the rest of the day chilling out with their buddies (just like professional footballers really!).

9 What was the catering like? Life in the great hall of Valhalla was one long round of feasting and drinking. The meat for the great feasts was served by the Valkyries and came from an enormous wild boar called Saehrimnir who was killed every day, then cut up and put in a huge cooking pot called Eldhrimnir (what's *yours* called?). After providing a fabulous nosh up for the hungry warriors, Saehimnir would obligingly and miraculously come back to life again so that he could be turned into gammon chops and pork pies for the following day. (The slower eaters weren't too keen on this trick as it tended to give them terrible indigestion.) The heroes washed down Saehrimnir with vast quantities of extra strength mead. Many warriors enjoyed drinking their mead from the skulls of their enemies (usually *after* they were dead).

10 What happened if you didn't manage to make it to Valhalla? Vikings who didn't die a heroic death in battle and just popped their clogs while they were in bed, taking the dog for a walk or sitting on the loo were said to have died a "straw death". They then spent all eternity in Hel which wasn't half as much fun as Valhalla. Some older Viking warriors who'd never actually got round to being killed in battle but were really desperate to get a slice of the Valhalla action would throw themselves on to their own spears. How they thought this could fool the Valkyries into believing they'd died a hero's death (rather than just being terminally sad) is anyone's guess!

Of course, the invention of the Valkyrie-Valhalla myth may have just been no more than a clever man-management tactic on the part of Viking chieftains who wished their warriors to give it everything they'd got on the battlefield.

LEGEND 7: THE THEFT OF IDUN'S APPLES

Have you ever had a really bad attack of "age fright"? You know the sort of thing don't you? You look in the mirror one morning and notice a couple of grey hairs, then immediately start to worry about whether your pocket money is going to be enough to provide you with a good pension and whether it's time to start stock-piling thermal underwear in readiness for your "twilight years".

No, of course you haven't! Getting old isn't the sort of thing young people normally bother about – they're too busy being youthful and vigorous and having lots fun! All that old age stuff can wait until you're really, really ancient can't it? (Maybe until even as late as your ... *twenty-first birthday*!) Getting old is something that does bother older people though. They go to all sorts of trouble to try and put it off – anti-wrinkle cream, jogging, vitamin pills, wardrobes full of wigs, stowing away on Club 18-30 holidays, the lot really! – but it always comes to them sooner or later.

The Viking gods were also a bit bothered about getting old ... but they weren't *too* bothered. That's because they had the Apples of Idun! These apples were brilliant – all the gods had to do was eat one a day and they stayed as youthful and full of beans (or apples?) as young people who were ... ooh, at least a *hundredth* of their age! The only problem was that one day the apples disappeared and the gods all began to age very, very rapidly indeed. It was definitely the sort of mystery that Inspector Norse might be called in to clear up! His intriguing report on the case is number seven in our ten best Viking legends.

An apple a day keeps the wrinkles away (an Inspector Norse mystery)

I was sitting in my office flipping through some back copies of "Amateur Defective" and thinking that things had been mighty quiet in the world of the gods just lately when there was a knock at the door.

"Come in!" I shouted. "And bring in the milk while you're at it!"

The door opened very slowly and I looked up to see this grey haired, wizened old guy (he must

have been at least eight hundred
and five if he was a day) stagger
in with my milk. The poor old
fogey looked as though he could
hardly stand, never mind carry a
couple of litres of semi-skimmed.

"Thanks!" I said, taking out my cash box. "Now,
how much do I owe you? And by the way, don't
you think a milk round is perhaps a bit ambitious
for someone of your age?"

"I'm not the milkman!" he croaked. "You just
asked me to bring it in!"

"Oh, so I did!" I said. "So who the Hel are you
then?"

"I'm Odin ... of course!" he moaned. "Don't you
recognize me, Norse?"

"Hey, guy!" I said. "Don't put me on! If you're
the great god Odin then I'm a wood elf's drawers!
I know Odin, he's a big tough god with shoulders
like an ox and a beard like a polar bear's
backside!"

"But I am Odin." he croaked pathetically.

There was something about him that seemed
vaguely familiar so I said, "OK! If you're Odin

 let's see you prove it!" and he
immediately pulled his spear from
its scabbard. "This is Gungnir, my
ace magic spear," he wheezed.
"Name your target!"

"See that that oak forest over

there?" I said, pointing to a distant mountainside. "Well, the third oak tree on the left is full of squirrels and the squirrel on the fourth branch from the top is holding an acorn and that acorn is being nibbled by a small and somewhat environmentally harmful caterpillar. I want you to waste that caterpillar. If you can do that I'll know you're Odin!"

Without hesitation the old guy hurled the spear through my open office window and moments

later I heard the terrified scream of a squirrel followed by the unmistakeable and deeply chilling death-rattle of a freshly disembowelled caterpillar ... and I knew this was Odin!

"Oh my god!" I said. "You really have let yourself go, haven't you Odin? How've you got yourself into this state? Too many mead and magic parties up at Gladsheim? And what do the other gods think?"

"It's not just me who is in this state!" said Odin. "All the other gods are like it too! We've all turned into wrinklies almost overnight. Handsome and powerful gods who've been in their prime for hundreds, if not thousands of years have become decrepit old bags of bones in just days. And it's worse for the goddesses.

"Before you could say, 'Pine needle wrinkle remover with added oil of muskrat, stacks of gorgeous, pouting glamour goddesses have turned into ancient, toothless old hags! And our memories have all begun to go as well. Sometimes we can't even ... er can't ... er...?"

"Manage to string the simplest sentence together?"

"Yes, and not only that! We've also begun to repeat everything we say! And we've started to repeat ourselves! Not to mention saying everything several times over!"

"But haven't you all been having your daily apple?" I said. "You know what they say "An apple of Idun a day keeps the wrinkles away!"

"We can't," he groaned. "The apples have disappeared!"

"Well, have a word with Idun then!" I suggested.

"We can't do that either!" he cried in despair. "She's disappeared too! That's why I've come to see you, Norse. I want you to find her and her apples quick sharp because if you don't there's no telling what ... err ... what...?"

"...will happen to you all?"

"Yes ... that as well!" he said.

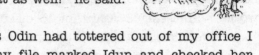

As soon as Odin had tottered out of my office I took out my file marked Idun and checked her out...

NAME :- Idun.

DESCRIPTION :- Maiden, as lovely as a spring morning. Usually to be seen wandering around Asgard giving fruit to grateful gods.

BACKGROUND :- Daughter of Ivaldi the earth dwarf. Wife of Bragi the god of poetry.

MOST NOTABLE POSSESSION :- A golden casket containing the Apples of Youth. Those who eat these apples will remain eternally young and zestful.

SPECIAL FEATURE OF CASKET :- No matter how many apples are taken it always stays full!

FAVOURITE SAYING :- "An apple a day keeps the wrinkles away!"

OTHERS SAID TO HAVE EXPRESSED AN INTEREST IN APPLES OF YOUTH :- The Giants.

"Ah, now there's a clue!" I thought to myself.

The next day I spoke to Odin again and asked him if anything odd had happened before Idun disappeared. He said the only thing he could remember that was slightly out of the ordinary had occurred during a jaunt that he'd taken to Midgard with Honir and Loki a few weeks earlier. He seemed reluctant to discuss the trip but nevertheless I asked him and the other two gods to pop into the office for a chat. On the appointed day only Odin and Honir turned up.

They said that Loki said he couldn't come because he'd got to wait in for the chariot repair man, or something like that? A glimmer of suspicion lit up a shady corner of my ever inert alert detective's brain. I then asked the two gods to talk about this trip and left my tape recorder running:

TAPE TRANSCRIPT –
Runesday 18th – interview held in office of Inspector Cathcart Norse

 Honir: Odin and Loki and me decided to go for a wander around Midgard. After hiking along the banks of a stream we got to feeling a bit peckish but realized that we'd left our sandwiches back in Asgard. At that moment we spotted a herd of oxen grazing at the water's edge and Loki said, "Hey guys, no problem, here's din-dins!" and he clobbered one of them lifeless while Odin and myself set about building a blazing wood fire. After we'd cut the ox up we began to barbecue the pieces over the flames. The delicious smell of roasting meat drove us all crazy!

 Odin: Yes, I'll never forget that smell – talk about mouth watering! We were absolutely starving, so the moment the meat looked brown and tender we pulled it off the coals but – believe it or not – it wasn't cooked! It was as raw as if it was still walking around the meadow. So we put it back on the flames and waited some more. Well, we waited and we waited, and every now and again we would take it off the fire to try it, but no matter how much we grilled it it still wouldn't cook!

Honir: "There's definitely something odd going on here!" said Loki. "I just don't what we've got to do to get this meat roasted."

"May I make a suggestion?" said a voice, and we looked up to see an enormous eagle sitting on a tree branch above us! "If you let me eat as much of that meat as I want before you have your share," continued the eagle, "I promise it'll be cooked in a jiffy! Just give me the word."

We looked at each other and shrugged our shoulders. Then Odin said, "Looks as if we've got no choice. I suppose half an ox is better than none?" And me and Loki nodded in agreement. The eagle flapped its wings a couple of times and some extra sizzling sounds came from the meat. Then the bird swooped down and set about tearing great chunks from the bones. The meat was done to a turn! The eagle must have been ravenous. It looked like it would scoff the lot before we got a taste!

It was all too much for Loki! He rushed at the eagle and cried "Oy, greedy gizzard, leave some nosh for us!" and gave it a thump on the rump with his walking stick.

The eagle didn't take kindly to this and with a couple of flaps of its wings it took off ... with the stick still attached ... and Loki hanging on, apparently unable to let go!

In no time at all the three of them were high above us. That's when the aerobatics display began. The eagle did the lot. Dives, swoops, loop the loops, not to mention some very spectacular dive bombing (with a smattering of poops!). All the time we could hear Loki screaming "Put me down you great overgrown feather duster, you!"

The end came after the eagle had done a couple of low-level sweeps across a field of painful looking thistles with Loki crying, "Ooh, ouch, oooh!" After that it dropped him into a bramble patch and we

ran to his rescue. All three of us then made our way back to Asgard feeling rather sorry for ourselves. As we'd all been made to look like fools and had handled the whole thing in a completely ungodlike manner we agreed to keep quiet about it. Which is why you're the first person to hear of it.

Seconds after the two geriatric gods had hobbled out of my office three things were uppermost in my computer-like brain...

1 Loki was reluctant to be interviewed. Why?

2 The giants had expressed an interest in Idun and her apples.

3 Loki was a devious character, notorious for being involved in treacherous escapades, scams and hypes, more often than not involving ... giants!

As I sat there pondering these intriguing facts there was a knock on my office door so I shouted "Enter!" and two humble looking chaps, whom I immediately recognized as servants of the god Heimdall, shuffled in.

"We've heard you're carrying out some sort of investigation linked to the disappearance of Idun and her apples," said the first one.

"That's right," I said.

"Well we've got some information that is ... hot, hot, hot!" said the second.

"Well, spill, spill, spill the ... beans, beans, beans!" I said.

"It is this, this, this!" said the first. "Just before all the gods began to go grey and saggy and lose their interest in nude table football and leap frog marathons, we saw Loki hurrying across Bifrost Bridge with Idun. And she was carrying her casket of apples!" said the first one.

"Wow, wow, wow!" I said.

"We feel this may be of importance to your enquiries." said the second one.

"So do I, I, I!" I said ... and decided it was time to bring in Loki.

Arresting Loki proved to be easier than I'd expected. Then again, I suppose the fact that the gods trussed him up like a turkey and played "Kick the Trickster" with him all the way up to my office may have had something to do with it. Even in their advanced state of senility those gods were still a pretty formidable bunch!

"So what happened, beaver breath?" I asked the snivelling wretch as he lay gibbering at my feet.

"Tell him the truth, Loki!" growled Odin, giving Gungnir a sharp twist. As Gungnir was already

wedged halfway up Loki's left nostril this naturally had quite a spectacular effect on the terrified wretch and he immediately began to confess. My tape machine was ready and running...

Ooh! Owch! Cripes! Stop. Stop! I'll tell everything. Hmm ... thath better...

Well ... it all started when that overgrown budgie picked me up and started doing aerobatics. Not many people know this, but I hate flying! Always have done. Unless I've got absolute control ... and in this case I hadn't!

"Glad to be able to give you a lift, Loki!" the eagle croaked as we soared to a thousand metres. "Anywhere I can drop you? How about those jagged rocks?"

I was terrified. I begged him to put me down.

He said he would – on one condition! "You must bring Idun and her apples to my place over in Jotunheim!"

"Hey, you're no bird!" I said "You're Thiassi, the giant, in your well-known eagle incarnation!"

"Well spotted!" said the eagle "Of course I'm Thiassi! You don't think an ordinary eagle would be capable of dreaming up a wicked scam like this did you? But more to the point, do you agree to my terms?"

It was an offer I couldn't refuse. Getting Idun out of Asgard was a piece of cake. She's not the brightest of goddesses is she? I lured her over Bifrost Bridge by telling her that I'd found a tree with apples that were much better than hers. As soon as we were well clear of Asgard I did a runner and left her to the mercy of Thiassi who – still in eagle shape – swooped down and whipped her off to Jotunheim along with her apples. And that's it guv'. It's a fair cop. You've got me bang to rights.

Now that Loki had confessed, my biggest concern was for Idun and her apples. Maybe those giants were doing something awful to her at that very moment. Or perhaps we were already too late! We had to act fast!

"Loki!" I said, "I am arresting you for aiding the abduction of Idun and her apples. But, having said that, I am giving you a chance to make amends."

"Oh no! Not more community service!" he groaned. "I just hate gardening!"

"No, not that, Loki!" I said. "At this moment Idun is in grave danger. Being a master of disguise and all manner of jiggery pokery, you are probably the only who can save her! Do that and we'll go easy on you!"

"Oh yeah! Way to go, Norse-man!" cried Loki." I swear you'll not regret this!"

And with that he borrowed Freyja's cloak of falcon feathers and hightailed it to Jotunheim.

As luck would have it, when he arrived at Thiassi's place, Idun was alone. He quickly turned her and her apples into a nut for convenience of transport and took off again. But he wasn't out of danger yet! Thiassi had spotted him and gave chase, once more in eagle shape. It began to look like he might just catch Loki before he could return his precious package to its rightful home! But Thiassi hadn't reckoned on Odin and the other gods. They were determined to prevent him stealing their precious fruit a second time and had built huge piles of wood shavings along the tops of Asgard's walls. As soon as Loki was safely over and Thiassi was in range they torched the lot.

Thiassi didn't stand an earthly! Before he knew it his tail feathers were alight and he was spiralling earthwards. The moment he hit the deck the gods piled in with their magic weapons. Result – one dead giant!

Final report

Core! I can't hear myself think for the sound of munching gods. They really do have some catching up to do with their fruit eating. Talk about a healthy appletite! But the wrinkles are going and they're all looking the picture of health once more as they all skip around Asgard like spring lambs! And I'm also pleased to say they've got their memories back. So they shouldn't have any problem remembering to give me the pay increase I've just put in for, should they?

FANTASTIC FACTS 7: WATCH OUT! THERE'S A FIEND ABOUT. TEN NORSE GIANTS AND MONSTERS TO AVOID

1 Angrboda (the distress-bringer). Angrboda was the big love of Loki's life – the *very* big love. She was his frost giantess girlfriend. Nowadays, the three children they produced would probably be locked up in a high security institution for young tearaways and made to play table tennis and computer games for the rest of their lives. Loki and Angrboda realized that their kids were a bit "different" so they kept them hidden in a cave. Odin eventually decided that the terrible tots presented such a potential threat to the gods that he had them all kidnapped. Their names were Hel, Jormungand and Fenrir. You can find out all about terrible Fenrir in Legend 8. Meanwhile, here's the low down on Hel and Jormungand…

2 Hel Loki and Angrboda's daughter Hel was actually quite nice looking – but only from the waist up. Her entire lower body was partially decomposed with great expanses of bone showing through the putrid, rotting flesh which hung limply from her legs and thighs (and made shopping for tights an absolute nightmare). Odin decided that he didn't want her around so he sent her down to the Underworld which (by some incredible coincidence!) also happened to be called Hel! She became the ruler, sitting on a throne known as the "Sick Bed" and generally lording it over people who'd died of illness and old age.

3 Jormungand This bloke must have been quite a disappointment to his mum and dad, not to say something of a surprise, as he was born in the form of a huge serpent with a forked tongue and green skin and even if you looked at him with your eyes half closed he was still absolutely revolting. Odin thought that Jormungand was a horrible child and he had him thrown into the sea. This turned out to be rather a bad idea as this new environment suited the repulsive creature right down to the ocean bed. He quickly grew so big that he was soon able to wrap himself right the way around the whole world and still have enough tail left over to put in his own mouth. He then became known as the Midgard Serpent and spent his time causing shipwrecks and being a general nuisance to the ocean-going Vikings.

4 Hymir This one was a rather grumpy frost giant who owned a massive beer-brewing cauldron which Thor acquired from him at great personal risk and inconvenience. Hymir was also the giant with whom

Thor once went fishing so that they could catch something to eat after Thor had polished off all the food in Hymir's house. Hymir caught two whales but Thor ended up hooking the sea monster, Jormungand, after baiting his fishing hook with the head of Hymir's black ox. There was a terrific tussle with Thor trying to pull Jormungand into the boat and Jormungand trying to pull Thor into the sea. All this excitement was too much for Hymir, who was actually something of a wimp, and at the crucial moment in the struggle he threw a wobbly and cut Thor's line, allowing evil Jormungand to escape. This annoyed Thor intensely but may well have been a relief to the Vikings as it meant they would still be able to carry on blaming their shipwrecks on Jormungand (rather than careless seamanship or sailing whilst under the influence of mead).

5 Geirrod This frost giant was one of Thor's worst enemies. When treacherous Loki was captured by Geirrod, he promised to bring Thor to him (minus his magic belt and hammer) in return for his own freedom. A friendly giantess called Grid warned Thor of Loki's treachery and lent him her own magic belt,

gloves and staff as protection against Geirrod. Thor used the gloves to catch a red hot iron ball which Geirrod

130

threw at him, then threw it back hitting the giant right in the bread basket, causing him considerable pain, shortly followed by considerable death!

6 Gjalp (the Howler) Gjalp was Geirrod's daughter. During Thor's visit to her dad's place she and her sister Greip tried to bump him off by suddenly lifting up his chair when he was snoozing and bashing his brains out on the ceiling. Quick(ish) thinking Thor jammed Grid's magic staff against the rafters and forced the chair back down, breaking the giantesses' backs and causing them really intense pain … shortly followed by really intense death!

7 Garm He was a really big and ferocious hound with a hairy chest that was always soaked in blood (not his own either!). Garm was the sort of dog who would let you down at Crufts Dog Show by snarling unpleasantly at all the other competitors and judges … then *eating* them! He belonged to Hel and his job was guarding her

front gates – though why anyone should want to try and break into such a horrible place in the first place is something of a mystery. Perhaps he was there to stop everyone breaking *out*? Garm was also known as the "Devil Dog".

8 Surt This fire giant was in charge of Muspell, the land of sparks and flames. Nowadays Surt would be described as a pyromaniac because of his fondness for setting light to anything he could put his flaming sword to. His big day came at Ragnarok, the end of the world, when he was given the job of torching the whole place. He would probably now be very pleased to know that he has his very own little bit of the world named after him. When volcanic eruptions between 1963 and 1967 caused a new island to form in the sea near Iceland, the authorities decided to name it Surtsey.

9 Nidhogg This chap was an entirely charmless and deeply repulsive dragon monster who lived in Niflheim, the lowest of the nine worlds. When he wasn't gnawing at one of Yggdrasil's roots he would pass his time ripping open the corpses of people who had been unlucky enough to end up in Hel. He also enjoyed sending the squirrel

Ratatosk up the tree with mischievous messages for the eagle who lived at the top (see page 22).

10 Skrymir This one was an extra *big* frost giant. A sort of mega-hyper-giant. Skrymir was ENORMOUS! One day when Thor and Loki were on their way to Utgard,

the giants' stronghold, they came across a vast hall. Deciding it was a convenient (if somewhat draughty) place to spend the night they kipped down in it, but were constantly disturbed by deafening roars and bone shaking vibrations. The next morning they got a terrific shock when they saw that they hadn't actually been sheltering in a hall but had been inside the thumb of Skrymir's empty glove! Yes, that's just how *big* he was! The roars and tremors had been caused by the snores of Skrymir himself who was sleeping near by! Later on Thor made a really big effort to bash in Skrymir's brains with Mjollnir while the massive bloke was asleep, but the giant merely woke up and asked if an acorn had fallen on his head. Yes, that's how *tough* he was! At the end of their adventure, after failing all sorts of tests of strength and skill, Thor and Loki discovered that Skrymir was actually Utgard-Loki, the King of the Giants. With the help of a bit of magic he'd kitted himself out in his mega-giant disguise and had been winding them up all along! Who says giants have no sense of humour?

LEGEND 8: THE BINDING OF FENRIR

Sometimes keeping pets can be a real nuisance can't it? Have you ever been troubled by a badly behaved animal? Maybe you've had to cope with a slightly stroppy goldfish … or a dangerously demented stick insect? This sort of animal can be a real pain, especially when you have to share your home with it each day. The Norse gods had just such an animal living with them in Asgard and its story is our eighth legend. It was slightly bigger than the average household pet – in fact, when it was fully grown, its jaws were said to be so big that the top one touched the sky and the bottom one touched the Earth! The terrible creature we're talking about was the huge wolf called Fenrir who, as you've already discovered, was related to Loki.

When the ancient Norsemen heard this tale of the problems caused by a giant wolf, it probably reminded them of their own fear of the packs of wolves that roamed the forests around their homes and the precautions they had to take to protect themselves from that ever present danger.

Troublesome Fenrir was the sort of creature that a modern day pet owner would probably seek expert advice about – maybe by writing to the advice pages of a publication like "Problem Pet". Come to think of it … perhaps the gods did something similar?

Dear Rolf,

I am writing to you from Asgard, home of the gods, for advice about something that has recently been giving us much cause for concern. Not long ago, one of our gods, Loki, and his giantess girl-friend, Angrboda, had a happy event and she gave birth to a bouncing bundle of joy! Except in this case the new arrival wasn't so little .... and was more a bundle of "JAWS" than of joy! This new baby – whose name is Fenrir – is really quite enormous and obviously takes after his mum in this respect. But that's not all – and this is where YOU come in, Rolf! This very odd child is covered in GREY FUR from head to foot and...rather than just lying in his pram and crying or gurgling happily like a normal infant, he seems much to prefer spending his time gnashing his teeth, licking his own bottom and howling at the moon! Rolf! Can you tell us – is this sort of thing "normal" for a three week old baby?

" To be quite honest with you we now suspect that Loki and Angrboda's new baby is not a little boy at all but some sort of "animal". This is why we have written to you! What do you think? Should we seek professional help?

We look forward to hearing from you
yours,
The gods

Dear gods!

I have given this matter my most careful consideration. And have I got news for you, mates! That's no child you've got there! It's a flippin' wolf that is… Or I'm a kangaroo's codpiece! If I were you, mates, I'd get that big bundle of furry fun enrolled in a course of puppy obedience classes quick sharp 'cos if you don't I think he might just turn into a bundle of furry fury and cause you terrible trouble in future. Listen! No matter how adorable these pesky pooches are when they're little, they all grow up into big hounds. So watch out, cobbers – or you'll end up *pet*'rified of him ... ha ha!

Yours *Rolf*

Dear Rolf,

We decided to take your advice and do something about bringing up young Fenrir properly but Loki got wind of our plans and hid him and a couple of his other (extremely peculiar) children in a cave. After some discussion we decided to take all of these infants into protective custody, both for their own good and the good of society in general. So we kidnapped them from their mountain hideaway. We have now got Fenrir here in Asgard where he is being looked after by the war god, Tyr, as he is the only one who can get near him (he's always been good with animals). You wouldn't believe the amount of meat Fenrir gets through —— he even eats more than Thor!! As a result he is growing at an amazing rate and is currently the size of a fully grown polar bear. Rolf —— is this normal for a two month old puppy?

               Best wishes,

                    The gods

Dear gods

No, it is not. (Or I'm a dingo's duodenum!)
Best of luck – it sounds like you're going to need it!

Rolf

Dear Rolf,

Help! Things are going from bad to worse! Fenrir is now as big as a small whale and is completely out of control. He bounds around Asgard doing exactly as he pleases, biting Valkyries, chasing chariots and generally frightening the wits out of everyone. The only time he calms down is when Tyr gives him his daily ton of walrus steaks. Yesterday he did a huge poo in the middle of Bifrost Bridge and caused a massive traffic jam (plus an even bigger stink!) He is a very naughty doggy indeed! What can we do?

Yours desperately

The gods

Dear gods,

You definitely slipped up by ignoring my advice about the obedience training didn't you? It strikes me that this wolf of yours is now beyond retraining … and just needs restraining. Get down to your local pet mart and pick up a lead now! Maybe a muzzle, too!

All the best,

Rolf

Dear Rolf,
   We took your advice and got Fenrir a huge chain to fasten him up good and proper. By the way — we decided to call the chain Laeding. When we put Laeding on him he was as good as gold and didn't even so much as raise a whimper. We obviously failed to notice the evil glint in his eye! The moment we were finished, he gave a playful yap, twitched his massive shoulders a couple of times and shattered the whole thing into a thousand pieces.

He then bounded off to resume his
reign of terror.

whatever can we do now?

yours

The Gods.

Dear gods,

I think you are in big, big trouble with this monstrous wolf creature of yours and really do need to take some drastic measures. In other circumstances I might have suggested bundling the mischievous mutt up in a very large bin liner along with a couple of large rocks and then dumping him in the nearest canal … or perhaps even throwing his favourite squeaky toy on to the fast lane of your local chariotway and then shouting "FETCH!". But, as this does not fit in with my image of chummy telly chap and caring animal lover, I won't.

You'll just have to get a stronger chain!!

Rolf

Dear Rolf,
We did as you said and got Fenrir an even stronger chain which we have called Droma. However, once again, all Fenrir had to do was flex his gigantic neck muscles and Droma too, fell to pieces.

He's off again digging up the neighbours' flower beds and chasing their reindeer up glaciers! We are at the end of our tethers (which is more than we can say for Fenrir!)

More advice needed!

The gods

Dear gods!

Have you thought of going to see the dwarves and asking them what they can come up with in the way of pooch restraint technology? I hear they're pretty handy with all matters technical.

Rolf

PS Your custom of giving names to dog leads is rather quaint isn't it? I can't say I've come across it before.

Dear Rolf,

We took your advice and sent our servant, Skirnir, to ask the dwarves what they could come up with. After extensive tests in their underground laboratories they've knocked up what they say is the ultimate dog collar.

HA HA

141

On the surface it appears to be nothing more than a bit of silky ribbon but its holding powers are said to be phenomenal. Those ever inventive dwarves tell us that they have incorporated all sorts of new "state of the art" materials into its manufacture, including mountain roots,

the sound of a cat's footsteps and the breath of a fish.... all topped off with a big dollop of good old bird spit! 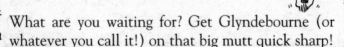 Do we try it (and risk more disappointment) or what?

yours
The gods

P.S. We have decided to call this one Gleipnir.

Dear gods!

What are you waiting for? Get Glyndebourne (or whatever you call it!) on that big mutt quick sharp!

Rolf

Dear Rolf,
Thank you, thank you, thank you! Good news! It's done! The beast is shackled! We have got Gleipnir on Fenrir and no matter how the great canine colossus twists

and turns and froths and
snaps and snarls he cannot
free himself from its
miraculous vice like grip!
Slobber jaws is well and
truly grounded at long
last! Hoorah!

But we have some
rather sadder news. Whilst we were putting
Gleipnir on Fenrir there was a rather unfortunate accident. As usual with matters
associated with the horrible hound, we asked
Tyr if he would lend a hand. When he saw
how terrified we all were of Fenrir he was
rather surprised and said he would
demonstrate to us the bond of love and
friendship and trust that existed between
him and the wolf. With a carefree cry of
"Look, chaps there's absolutely nothing to
worry about at all, he really is a great
big softy!" he thrust his hand
into the massive beast's open
mouth ... and Fenrir immediately
bit it off! Just like
that! (Oooh ... owch!) Well ...
... talk about laugh! I can tell
you Rolf we were in tucks. It's
the funniest thing we've seen since the
day Odin got his beard caught in his
chariot wheel. When we had all finished
rolling around on the floor and splitting

our sides, Loki said (between sniggers) "That's
...not quite what we meant when we...
ha ha... said we wanted you to LEND
A HAND, Tyr....ha ha ha!" and we all
burst into fits of laughter again. (He
is a wag that Loki!) For some reason
Tyr didn't seem to find this joke the
slightest bit funny!?

Best wishes and once again thank
you for your advice.

yours gratefully

The gods.

P.S. There is one more thing you can
perhaps help us with. Since we have got
Fenrir tied up he does nothing but
howl and howl all day and
night. It's driving us all
nuts, Any ideas?

Dear gods!
Look! I am getting well miffed with your constant
pathetic letters. Are you lot thick, or what??!! Just
wedge his gob open with a spear or something!!

Rolf

Dear Rolf,
The spear trick worked a treat.
We haven't had a peep out of him since

Now just one more thing... and we promise you this is definitely the last you will hear from us!

Odin seems to think that one day (probably some-time around the end of the world) Fenrir will escape from Gleipnir's grip and then wreak a terrible revenge on us all.

What do you think?

The gods.

Dear whingers,

I sincerely hope he does!

Rolf

FANTASTIC FACTS 8: NORSE CREATURES GREAT AND SMALL

The ancient Norsemen came into contact with all sorts of animals each day of their lives. Some, like the wolves, were a nuisance. But others, like pigs and goats and oxen, were really useful. The Vikings depended on them for survival! They made their clothes from them, used them for transport and, most importantly of all, they ate them! (Old Norse saying: veggie Viking = dead Viking!) So, it's not surprising that, as well as featuring the big bad creatures like Fenrir, some of the legends are also about some extremely talented and helpful animals too, as you'll find out.

1 Toothgnasher and Toothgrinder: Thor's really "fast" food

You already know that Toothgnasher and Toothgrinder, Thor's huge goats, pulled his chariot and helped provide the astonishing sound effects that we know as thunder. What you may not know, is that Thor occasionally turned these four-footed friends of his into lunch! Whenever he felt like some nosh, but was fresh out of reindeer steaks or caribou cutlets, he would simply clobber the goats to death then gobble them up! But he always made sure he left their skin and bones completely unharmed. Then, the next day he would simply wave his magic

146

hammer over their remains and they'd miraculously reform into good old Toothgnasher and Toothgrinder, complete with all their body bits. Not even complaining of so much as a headache or a set of nastily nibbled knick-knacks, they'd instantly be as right as rain and rarin' to get back to some serious chariot pulling!

2 Gullinkambi: the alarm "cock" of Valhalla

Valhalla, the hall of the dead warriors, had its own early morning wake up service in the shape of a cockerel called Gullinkambi. As each day dawned Gullinkambi would throw back his head and do an ear shattering COCK-A-DOODLE-DOO! This was the signal for the dead warriors to jump out of bed and start belting the living daylights out of each other (or out of Gullinkambi, if they had any sense!). Gullinkambi's other claim to fame was that he would be the one to do the COCK-A-DOODLE-DOO that would warn the gods that Ragnarok, the end of the world, was about to take place.

3 Gulltop, the Wonder Horse

Freyr, the fertility god, and confusingly named brother of the goddess Freyja, owned an amazing horse called Gulltop. Gulltop had all sorts of talents but his most useful ones were the ablity to gallop through fire and see in the dark (but he never ever discussed his hopeless addiction to fresh carrots). Gulltop came in particularly useful when Freyr wanted to send a message to Gerd, a giantess he fancied. Not wanting to risk a trip to giant-land himself he lent Gulltop to his servant Skirnir, who nipped off to Jotunheim for him. Gulltop made short work of the ring of icy fire that surrounded Gerd's place and in no time at all Skirnir was able to deliver his message to her, something like, "Ay, my boss wants to know if you'll go out with him?". Not long after this, Gerd got together with Freyr in Asgard and the two of them lived happily ever after for quite some time (aarh).

4 Ottar: the goddess Freyja's toy boar

Freyr's gorgeous sis', Freyja, had a human sweetheart called Ottar. Ottar wanted to visit a giantess called Hyndla so he could have a drink of her special beer that helped you remember things really well. Before they set out on the journey, Freyr decided to go the whole hog and turned Ottar into a huge wild boar called Hildisvini, then rode him to Hyndla's place. She also occasionally used Ottar to pull her chariot (perhaps

148

when it was the cat's day off?).

Boaring Fact - During the eighth century AD, Viking warriors wore helmets with a wild boar decoration on them to show respect for Hildisvini.

5 Ratatosk: the gossip squirrel

Ratatosk was the squirrel who lived in Yggdrasil, The World Tree. It got it's thrills from hanging around the eagle who lived in the top of the tree and listening out for any insulting comments it might make about Niddhogg, the dragon who lived at the bottom of the tree. It would then dash down to Niddhogg and tell it what the eagle had said. After that it would wait for Niddhogg to say something awful about the eagle, so it could dash back up the tree to tell the eagle what the dragon thought of it. It spent its whole pathetic life doing this! Remind you of anyone?

6 Skinfaxi and Hrimfaxi: the Norse horses who served ... both day and night

Skinfaxi (whose other other name was Shining Mane) was the horse that galloped around the sky pulling the chariot driven by Dag (Day). The glow from Skinfaxi's shining hairdo lit up all the heavens and the earth. In fact it might well be providing the light that *you* are reading by at this very moment! While Skinfaxi did the "Day" shift, its pal Hrimfaxi (whose other name was Frosty Mane) did the "Night" shift – by pulling the chariot driven by Day's mother, who was called Nott (Night)! If you look on the grass in the evening or early in the morning you may see the froth from Hrimfaxi's mouth. It's the stuff that boring people call dew.

7 The remarkably useful ox-sons of Gefion

The goddess Gefion may well have enjoyed telling everyone that her sons were as strong as oxen ... because they *were* oxen. Gefion was the goddess of ploughing so it was a really fortunate coincidence for her when she got together with a giant and managed to produce these four strapping beasts. One day, when Gefion was having a walk round Asgard disguised as a beggar woman, she bumped into the King of Sweden, who was also in disguise (walking around in disguise was a really popular pastime in those days). Gefion shared her food and fire and a few other things with the king and he was so grateful for her favours that he said something like, "I say, old wrinkly. I am the King of Sweden and I'm right pleased with *you*! *You* can have as much of my kingdom as you can plough in a day and a night!" "Hmm, just the job for my lads!" thought Gefion, and she nipped to Sweden with her four sons and got ploughing. After one day and night they'd ploughed a massive area of land which they then floated across the sea and anchored next to to Denmark. It is the island that is now known as Zealand. (Treat this geographical theory with caution!)

8 Heidrun: the mead goat of Valhalla

Odin's pet goat, Heidrun, was a sort of walking beer keg. She provided an everlasting supply of mead for the dead heroes in Valhalla so that when they came in from a hard day's scrapping they could get completely off their faces without even having to nip down to the off-licence or open their wallets. Golden five-star mead gushed straight from her teats into the barrel which they all filled their horn mugs from. Cheers nanny!

9 Hugin and Munnin: Odin's spies in the sky

When Odin sat on his big tall seat in Asgard keeping

151

tabs on everything that was going on in the worlds he never had to worry missing anything when he turned his back (or nipped to the loo). His two pet ravens, Huginn (whose name means Thought) and Muninn (whose name means Memory) acted as his "spies in the sky". They spent their days flapping around the worlds and sticking their beaks into everyone's business. On returning to Asgard, they would perch on Odin's shoulders and whisper into his ear about everything they'd seen. Hence the phrase "a big black bird told me"!

The Vikings themselves found ravens very useful birds. They took them with them on their long sea voyages and sent them off in search of land. The birds would instinctively fly in the direction of the land and the Vikings would follow.

10 Skoll and Hati: the seriously dysfunctional space wolves

Skoll and Hati were a pair of very big wolves. They came from the Iron Wood down on Earth, and were the children of an ancient and mysterious giantess. If they'd lived nowadays they'd be chasing cars and old men on bikes and would be taken to see an animal psychiatrist or humanely put to sleep. But, as they were legendary wolves who also knew how to defy the laws of gravity they charged around after *much* bigger targets. Hati's job was chasing after the Moon while Skoll's was chasing the Sun. They eventually played an important part in the end of the world.

TEN "PHENOMENALLY" PUZZLING VIKING BRAIN TEASERS

As well as reminding the Vikings of the wolves that they feared so much, the legend of Fenrir also stood for many of the other dangers that threatened them. They knew that there were many things in the world that were far more powerful than themselves and that dangerous natural forces were extremely unpredictable. They never did know just when a catastrophe was likely to strike!

What made things worse was that they probably didn't have much idea of the actual causes of these frightening occurrences. In order to make sense of lots of "completely baffling" happenings in Nature, the ancient Norse decided that they were all caused by the gods and giants and nature spirits, rather than trying to arrive at some sort of scientific explanation. In the late twentieth century it's quite hard to believe that, on spotting a rainbow, your average Viking in the valley would immediately think "Ah! There's the Bifrost Bridge!

That wonderful multi-coloured miracle of modern engineering lovingly created by our glorious gods so that they can conveniently cross from their world to ours! It really is quite fabulous!" Mind you, it's a bit weird thinking, "Hmm ... yes. That's a rather superb example of the refractive, prismatic effect of sunlight on water droplets."

Here's your chance to wipe away the effects of about a thousand years worth of knowledge and scientific research ... not to mention tons of brilliant books and "Wonderful World of Nature" type telly programmes! See if you can make your brain go "ancient Norse" and match these natural occurrences to their mythical causes.

The natural phenomena

1 The cracking of the ice in glaciers and the roar of distant avalanches.
2 Vast, towering, unexplored mountain ranges.
3 Sunlight.
4 Moonlight.
5 Deep chasms and crevasses.
6 The rumble of thunder.
7 Echoes that occur naturally in mountainous areas.
8 Lightning.
9 Gale force winds.
10 Volcanoes.

The causes

a) Turbulent air currents caused by Odin racing across the sky on Sleipnir.

b) The light from the frosted mane of a horse which pulled a chariot driven by the kidnapped son of a human being.

c) Giants who've stayed out all night, forgotten to go home and been turned to stone by the early morning light.

d) The light from the glowing mane of a horse which pulled a chariot driven by the kidnapped daughter of a human being.

e) Dwarves hiding behind rocks and whispering (only at night, of course!).

f) Frost giants partying or having family rows.

g) Damage caused by clumsy giants when the earth was first being made.

h) Fire giants blowing their tops!

i) The noise made by the wheels of Thor's chariot rumbling on clouds as he charged across the sky.

j) The sparks and flashes caused by Thor striking rocks with his hammer Mjollnir.

Answers:
1f)
2c) The giants had the same problem as the dwarves – they were said to be petrified by daylight (according to some versions of the legend, anyway!).
3d) & 4b) The gods originally created the bright bits in the heavens (sun, moon, stars … that sort of thing) from sparks that happened to shoot out of the fiery land of Muspell. However, one day a human man living down in Midgard had the cheek to name his children Sun and Moon. He (rather confusingly) called his son Moon, and his daughter Sun! The gods didn't like this one bit (they would have far preferred Dwayne and Lisa) so they immediately snatched the kids and gave them the full-time and extremely demanding job of steering the chariots that guide the sun and moon through the sky. Moon leads the way and Sun follows close behind him. They are constantly pursued by two gigantic wolves called Skoll and Hati who will eventually catch them and eat them – but not in our lifetime (thank godness).
5g)
6i) The Vikings believed that every time they heard the sound of thunder it was actually the noise of the wheels of Thor's chariot rumbling across the clouds (but if they heard it on cloudless day they knew it would just be the roar of a passing Jumbo jet).
7e) The dwarves were notorious gossips.
8j)
9a) Odin dashed about the sky hunting for the evil god Loki
10h)

LEGEND 9: THE DEATH OF BALDER

Parents can be very fussy can't they? *"Don't do this! Be careful of that! Don't put your head in that lion's mouth. Don't swim in that tank of raw sewage. Don't go over Niagara falls on that tea tray!"* On and on they go!

Some parents, like the Norse god Balder's mum, take this sort of thing so seriously that they become what's known as "over protective". Frigg worried about Balder constantly and went to amazing lengths to make sure that no harm came to him. Then again, she probably had good reason to! Balder was forever having these really gruesome nightmares in which he foresaw terrible things happening to him and when he told his mum about them she got into a right old tizzy. Unfortunately, despite all her efforts to protect him, poor old Balder still ended up meeting a very sticky end indeed in the legend that's number nine in our top ten. His death caused a huge kerfuffle in the world of the gods and, what's worse, it actually led to a real mega-disaster a bit later on.

Of course, there was treachery and mischief involved in the whole affair of Balder's death and the culprit was eventually caught and punished. If it had happened in modern times it would certainly have led to the sort of huge and completely gripping courtroom drama that has the whole world on the edge of its seat!

The court case of the age: The trial of Balder's killer

Judge: Call the first witness – Frigg, mother of Balder.

State prosecutor: Frigg, in your own words, tell us how this tragic affair all started.

Frigg: Well, I'd been anxious about my boy for weeks. You know the way us mums fret. He'd been having these really gruesome nightmares in which he foresaw his own death and, as you can imagine, I was beside myself with worry. There was only one thing for it! I got out there and had a personal word with all the things in the world that could possibly do him injury … ice, fire, sharp objects, fast moving chariots, forked lightning, tiny fish-bones that might get stuck in his throat … the lot really! And I got them all to swear not to harm a hair of my lad's head. Being a goddess does have its advantages you know – or so I thought! Sob … sob…

Judge: Call the next witness – Hermod, son of Odin, brother of Balder and god of errands.

State prosecutor: Hermod, please tell us about these "games" you played with Balder.

158

Hermod: When us other gods discovered that Balder had become completely death- and injury-proof we were right tickled and just couldn't resist having a bit of a laugh with him – we're only "god-like" after all, aren't we? It started off with Thor taking a couple of pokes at him with a sharp stick but, when we saw it had no effect on him, things got a bit wild! Before we knew it we were knocking six bells out of him, and bashing Balder quickly got to be a real craze with all of us. We really looked forward to it! And the amazing thing was it didn't have the slightest effect on him! Sometimes when we got a bit *too* carried away and were giving him an extra thorough doing over we'd get a bit worried and stop to ask if the pain was getting to him. "What pain?" he'd reply with a grin. "Didn't feel a thing!" And then we'd all laugh and throw him off the top of a cliff!

Anyway, this went on for weeks and weeks until the terrible day of the darts tournament. You see, we'd invented this brilliant new variation on darts using Balder as the board. We'd got ourselves into teams and we were all very excited. Well ... you know what happened next! In the midst of all the throwing and cheering someone (I didn't see who) lobs a wooden spear or somethin' and down Balder goes. He didn't move, so Thor went over to him and shook him and said, "Come on, Balder, buddy, stop winding us up! We've got a darts match to finish." But he still didn't move and that's when we knew that he was really dead!

State prosecutor: Frigg, during the time that your son (supposedly) couldn't be affected by harmful things, did anything occur that you later thought of as suspicious or in the slightest bit unusual?

Frigg: Well, yes now I come to think of it there was something. A few weeks after I'd made Balder peril-proof, a wrinkled old crone called at my hall and asked me for directions to Bifrost Bridge. During the course of our conversation the ancient hag happened to mention that she'd just seen a gang of gods knocking the stuffing out of a rather good-looking god who just grinned pleasantly all the time as they all did their best to turn him into minced mortal. I explained to her that that was my son Balder and she needn't worry as it was just the chaps having one of their Balder-battering sessions. When I told her about how I'd protected him from all the possible harm that could befall him she became extremely interested and wanted to know if I'd made absolutely sure that I'd spoken to every single thing in the worlds that could possibly do Balder any harm. And that's when I remembered about the mistletoe.

State prosecutor: The mistletoe?

Frigg: Yes, the mistletoe. I was on my way back from

my mission to ask everything in the world not to harm my lad when I noticed the mistletoe and suddenly remembered that I hadn't got it to agree. At the time

I was feeling extremely tired after my exhausting trip and I thought to myself, "So what! It's only a bit of mistletoe and I really am absolutely cream crackered. I'm sure it won't hurt to give it a miss!", and I thought no more about it. Oh, if only I'd known … sob, sob, sob.

Judge: Call Hod, brother of Balder!

State prosecutor: Hod … is it true that you are blind?

Hod: Yes sir … as a bat!

State prosecutor: And is it true you threw the spear that killed your brother?

Hod: To be honest, sir, I'm not entirely sure. I was sort of hanging around at the back of the hall during the darts match wishing I could join in the fun when this really creepy voice at the side of me said, "Don't you wish you could have some fun too, Hod?" and I said "Yes," and the voice said, "Well, you can just cop hold of this here spear, mate, and I'll point your arm in the right direction, then all you have to do is fling it when I give the word!" So I did, and next moment I heard this groan and the sound of a body hitting the floor and then there was a right to-do! Next thing I heard someone say "Oh Hod, now see what you've gone and done!" … which I thought was a bit insensitive considering the circumstances.

State prosecutor: Could you identify the voice of the person who gave you the spear if you heard it again?

Hod: Yes, I could.

State prosecutor: I will now return to witness Hermod. Hermod, please tell us what happened next

Hermod: Once we'd realized that Balder really had popped his clogs we were all very, very cut up indeed. So, as soon as Odin said, "Anyone fancy going down to the Netherworld and seeing if they can persuade Hel to let my lad back into the world of the living?" I volunteered straightaway. Dad was so grateful that he even lent me Sleipnir for the journey and as a result I was off like a shot. I made good time and finally, after nine nights of riding through a valley that was so dark that I couldn't even see Sleipnir beneath me, I arrived at the gates of Hel.

Talk about horrific! I peered through the iron bars and found myself face to face with hundreds of poor lost souls. They were all staring out at me, their faces twisted in agony as they groaned and gibbered and writhed in torment, splashing around in steaming hot pools of their own vomit and gnawing savagely at each other's flesh! It was horrible! What a way to end up! I really do feel sorry for them ... it must be absolute Hel down there!

Anyway, all of a sudden, I saw Balder sitting high above all these poor wretches with this really sad look on his face and I waved to him and yelled "Yo, brudder ... how goes it?" and he gave me one of those winning smiles of his and said, "Not so bad, Hermod,  all things considered!" That was Balder for you! Always trying to look on the bright side! Suddenly I smelled this real bad smell and heard this terrible wheezing sound – very asthmatic – and there was Hel standing right next to me! "So what do you want messenger boy?" she snarled.

"Balder!" I said. "We want him back. *Everyone* wants him back!

"Right!" she said. "I'll make a deal! You prove to me that all things in the world love Balder as much as you say they do and you can have him back! If every single thing in the nine worlds sheds tears for him then I will allow him to return to Asgard!"

Of course, I immediately rushed back to Asgard to tell Dad what she had said.

Judge: Call Odin!

State prosecutor: Odin, what did you do when Hermod

brought you the news of Hel's deal?

Odin: I sent my messengers out into the world. Through them, I commanded all things to weep for Balder, and they did. All the gods and the giants and the animals and the trees and the dwarves and the elves ... they all wept ... everyone and everything! There was a right wailing and gnashing of teeth I can tell you! Even the mountains were sobbing their rocks off! So, naturally, I thought Hel would be bound to let him go. And then I got bad news! A messenger returned and told me that he had visited an old frost giant called Thokk in his cave and when he'd asked him to weep for Balder he'd replied, "No way, Hosé!" and then told him to take a running jump into a bottomless crevasse. Despite the messenger's pleadings, the giant just refused to sob. And that, sir, is why my son will remain in Hel for ever more!

Judge: That sad note brings me to my summing up. The evil wretch who you (should) see before you in the dock has been identified as... 1) The old crone who stopped at Frigg's hall. 2) The conniving reprobate who gave Hod a  spear made out of mistletoe wood – the very thing that Frigg failed to protect Balder from – then persuaded him to throw it at his own brother with such tragic consequences. 3) The evil-doer who turned himself into the giant called Thokk who refused to weep for Balder, thus causing him to remain in Hel for evermore. That wretch is none other than ... LOKI ... the Trickster himself! Foreman of the jury how do you find him?

Jury: Err we don't ... he's not there, is he?

Judge: Well that's as may be. Unfortunately, as the accused was being escorted to the courthouse by Securigod he managed to slip away and hasn't been seen since. Nevertheless I must ask you to say how you find him.

Jury: Guilty m'lud – definitely guilty!

To sum up! Loki did do a runner when the gods realized that it was him who had so cruelly condemned Balder to a lifetime in Hel. But it wasn't too long before they managed to capture him and organize a suitably unpleasant punishment, as you'll find out from our next facts section. And what about poor old Hod? Well despite the fact that he really had been an unwitting accomplice in the death of his brother, the gods still seemed to hold him partly responsible for the tragedy. Some time later Odin got together with his third wife Rinda and they had a son called Vali. Not long after his birth – and no doubt to the great delight of his parents – one of the first things that little Vali did was to kill Hod and send him to join Balder in Hel.

FANTASTIC FACTS 9: THE LOKI PROFILE

As you will have no doubt realized by now, Loki was the all time bad boy of the Viking Legends. And there are more stories about him than about any of the other gods. This is probably because most people prefer hearing tales of rogues rather than boring "goody goodies". If you don't believe it, take a look at what's on TV this week! There were many sides to Loki's character. To give you a complete picture of this "ultimate" rascal we've created this Loki personality profile. Maybe he'll bring to mind someone you know? But let's hope not!

The ten faces of the "bad boy" of the Viking legends

1 Serial husband Loki was a fabulously handsome, witty and lively god, so, rather than squander his talents and charms on just one woman, he had three partners altogether. The first was the prettily named Glut. His second partner was Angrboda, the giantess – you already know about her, and the lovely children they produced. His third was the beautiful, kind and pure hearted Sigyn. Loki definitely didn't deserve

166

her, but for some reason she was utterly devoted to the conniving Trickster, as you'll find out a bit later. Maybe in addition to being mind-bogglingly good looking, she was also mind-bogglingly dim?

2 Charming entertainer
One day a beautiful giantess turned up at Asgard. The giantess was Skadi, the daughter of Thiassi. He's the giant the gods bumped off at the end of the Idun's Apples caper. She was absolutely hopping mad about the death of her dad and demanded a life in exchange for his. The gods offered her gold in compensation but she refused it and insisted that they give her the life of one of their own kind.

Try as they might they couldn't come up with a way of getting themselves out of this predicament. Then, just as things were beginning to look really grim, Loki stepped in and saved the day! Turning on his devastating charm, and making good use of his well known talents to amuse, he began to dance for Skadi. Little by little, a smile began to break out on the face of the stroppy giantess, and by the time Loki had finished capering and cavorting the great big babe was laughing fit to burst! Loki's performance put her in such a mood that she abandoned her demand for a life and instead agreed to marry the god with the prettiest feet in

Asgard – who turned out to be Njord, the sea-god.

3 Working class hero A giant called Skrymsli won a peasant's son off him in a game of chess. The peasant asked the gods to help him get his son back but despite the best efforts of Odin and Hoenir they couldn't rescue him. Finally the peasant asked crafty Loki, who immediately turned the boy into an egg hidden inside a fish. The giant caught the fish and was busy sorting through its eggs for the one that was really a peasant when Loki turned it back into the lad. "Run for it son…!" he said to him. "But as you do, make sure you go '*through the boathouse*'!" The boy did as he was told and escaped. The giant dashed through the boathouse after him, just as Loki had planned, and did himself a nasty mischief on the huge spikey trap the Trickster had set for him. Loki then ran in and chopped off one of the giant's legs but unfortunately the leg immediately grew back on by magic so Loki chopped off the other leg. This time he took the precaution of sticking a bit of flint and steel between the leg and the giant's body. This stopped the magic working and the giant then bled to death (ha ha!). As a result of this daring rescue and Loki's association with firesides, comfort and fun, the Viking peasants thought he was top of the gods (but that's peasants for you!).

4 Treacherous "friend"
One day Loki was wandering around wearing Freyja's falcon skin when the evil giant Geirrod caught him. When Geirrod asked Loki who he really was, the crafty god refused to tell him so the giant shut him in a box and said he could stay there for ever. Loki promised Geirrod that he would bring Thor to him completely unarmed if only he would release him from the box. Geirrod was

GO ON! BOX YER WAY OUT OF THAT THEN!

delighted with the idea of having Thor at his mercy so he let Loki go. Thor loved being with lively Loki, so when the Trickster said to him, "Hey Thor! Let's go to Midgard. I've set up a double date with a couple of gorgeous chicks! *And* there's no need to bring Mjollnir. It's a fun trip!", the dopey thunder god agreed without hesitation. This led to Thor's very narrow escape from Geirrod and his revolting daughters which you've already read about.

5 Cunning thief Odin told Loki to steal Freyja's necklace, Brisingamen. Loki made himself very small so he could squeeze through a crack to get into Freyja's bedroom. She was wearing Brisingamen, but was sleeping in a position that made it impossibe for him to unclip the fastener so he turned himself into a flea

and gave her a bite on the bosom. This caused Freyja to roll over, making it easy for him to swipe the necklace. He then turned back into his old self and took the necklace to Odin (well, that's what happens in one version of the tale). In another version, Heimdall, the god who guards the Rainbow Bridge, sees Loki steal the necklace and challenges him. They have a bit of tussle and Loki is finally persuaded to give it back to Freyja. So take your pick!

6 Cruel and mocking joker Loki loved to mock and insult everyone else. Winding up the world seemed to give him the greatest of pleasure. He called Bragi, the god of poetry, a big softie. When poor old Tyr had his hand bitten off by Fenrir the mega-wolf, Loki was the god who laughed loudest. He accused the goddesses Iduna, Gefion, Frigg and Sif of flirting and being

unfaithful to their hubbies. He told Heimdall, the god who guarded Bifrost, that he was nothing more than a mere servant of all the other gods. He even mocked Odin by calling him a "woman" when the boss god once turned himself into a witch.

7 Cold blooded murderer
Loki went to Midgard with Odin and Thor. They watched an otter catching a salmon in a river. Loki threw a stone at the otter and killed it. After they'd eaten the salmon and Loki had skinned the otter, the gods went and asked a farmer called Hreidmar if they could spend the night in his house. During the night Hreidmar and his sons, Regin and Fafnir, tied the gods up. Then Hreidmar told them that he was really a magician who turned one of his sons into an otter each day so that they could go fishing. The otter that Loki had killed had been Hreidmar's son! (Uh oh!) He told the gods they must give him lots of gold in compensation for the boy's life or he would keep them prisoner for ever! Loki was set free, and quick as a flash he nipped off to the bottom of the ocean where he met a dwarf called Andvari who had masses of gold. Loki very kindly offered not to strangle Andvari to death, in exchange for his loot! Andvari very sensibly agreed and

171

Loki made off with all Andvari's gold *and* his best gold ring. Andvari was well miffed about all this, so he put a curse on whoever owned the ring and the gold. Loki handed the gold to Hreidmar and the gods were allowed to go on their way. Of course, none of this did Hreidmar and his lads any good because Andvari's curse brought them nothing but trouble for the rest of their lives!

8 Ruthless gatecrasher After the death of Balder, Aegir, the sea-god, threw a party to try and cheer all the other gods up but didn't invite Loki (surprise, surprise!). Nevertheless, Loki still turned up and gatecrashed the whole shebang. The moment he was inside he characteristically set about making himself thoroughly unpopular by murdering one of Aegir's servants and telling all the other gods what a lot of idiots and good-for-nothings they were. He then went on

to insult Freyja by talking about her fondness for having hordes of boyfriends ... all at the same time! This all became too much for Thor, who blew his top and threatened to hammer Loki to death on the spot. Loki made his excuses and left!

9 Desperate fugitive After Aegir's party the gods decided that enough was enough and set out to bring Loki to justice. Realizing his number was up, Loki went into the mountains and hid out next to the tumbling

stream which was to be his final escape route. His plan was to turn himself into a salmon and swim out to sea if necessary. It occured to him that the gods might make a really strong net with which to capture him. He was so desperate to avoid capture that he decided to make just such a net himself so he could check out how effective it was. This proved to be his downfall! The gods had already discovered his hiding place and were actually on their way up there at that very moment. Just as he finished the net, Loki spotted them and immediately burned his handiwork. He then turned into a salmon and jumped into the stream. As soon as the gods arrived at his den they spotted the tell tale ashes of the net and put two and two together. After some exciting splishing and sploshing in the stream they captured him in their own net and took him off to be punished.

10 Wretched prisoner Once Loki was back to his old shape after his capture from the stream the other gods set about punishing him for all his wicked deeds. The first thing they did was kill Narvi, one of Loki's sons from his marriage to Sigyn. In a stomach-churning display of creative cruelty they ripped out poor Narvi's guts and used them to tie his dad to some rocks in a cave (urrgh!). They then pulled their masterstroke! Taking the most deadly poisonous snake they could lay their hands on they fastened it to a stalactite just above Loki's head so that the hot stinging poison from its fangs would drip directly onto his face (nice one gods!). This is where good Sigyn showed her undying (and totally gormless?) devotion to her suffering husband. Seizing a handy bowl she caught the drips. Of course, because the snake had a never-ending

supply of venom, this meant that she would be forever rushing backwards and forwards between Loki and the spot where she emptied the disgusting stuff. And in between dashes Loki would have to endure the steady drip onto his exposed mush.

Loki remained like this almost until the End Of The World – but then he escaped and caused even more chaos than ever. You can read all about *that* absolute nightmare in Legend Ten … our next and last story!

LEGEND 10: RAGNAROK

Our tenth legend is the story of the end of the world as told in the Viking legend of Ragnarok. The ancient Norse really did believe that the end of the world would come sooner or later and when it did they were expecting Hel to break loose (accompanied by lots and lots of her evil friends!). As you may have noticed, their gloomy prophecy has not yet come true. Let's hope the ancient Viking legend makers were wrong!

If television had been around in the days of the Viking legends, the TV news makers would have been delighted with the arrival of this catastrophe to end all catastrophes. It would have given them a brilliant excuse to go completely over top with all those breathless on the spot reports, interviews and news flashes they get so carried away with whenever anything big and bad happens. And Ragnarok certainly was, *very* big ... and *very* bad!

PRESENTED BY

JEREMY AXEMAN

Jeremy Axeman: Goood eeevening! Here at Bad Newsnight we've been getting reports of all sorts of strange goings on throughout Midgard. What's more, there've been some very nasty outbreaks of violence between peasants, or "thralls" as we call them here. So! What *is* it all about? We sent our roving reporter Nora Weejanbod to investigate.

Nora Weejanbod: Hello! I'm in a field somewhere in Midgard. I'm with a Mr N. Thrall and his best friend, Dismal Thrall. We're looking at a dead cow! Mr Thrall, where did it come from?

N. Thrall: Oi dunno. Dismal here reckons it must have dropped out of the sky!

Dismal Thrall: Yes! Yes! I'm sure it did. It is a portent of doom!

N.Thrall: No it's not ... it's a dead cow!

Dismal Thrall: There is evil about in the world! I feel it in my bones. There is bad feeling between comrades and kinfolk alike.

N.Thrall: You're talking out of your bottom, flabby features.

Dismal Thrall: No I'm not! Take *that*, pudding guts!

N.Thrall: You want some, do you? Well, cop *this* then, tombstone teeth!

Nora Weejanbod: Oh dear, the Thralls have begun to fight! They're going at it hammer and tongs. And now their families are joining in! It's turning into a real free for thralls. Ooh! I say, mind my microphone! This is Nora Weejanbod returning you to the studio. Ooh ... Owch ... Hey, do you mind!

Jeremy Axeman: Hmmm, veeairy strange? Neeeeeow... I've got our resident expert, Ann Expert, with me. I'm going to ask her to explain what's going on. Ann! What's going on?

Ann Expert: Well Jeremy, ever since the death of the people's prince, a really bad atmosphere has set in throughout society. People are all really ratty and crabby and...

Jeremy Axeman: By the "people's prince", I take it you mean Balder?

177

Ann Expert: Yes, of course I do, weasel-wits! Now, where was I? Yes, reported cases of chariot-rage and goat abuse have increased alarmingly in recent months. Balder, that model of perfect goodness, was a real inspiration to all the decent folk in the world. We
now fear that the terrible inter-human tension following his death will finally erupt into…

Jeremy Axeman: All out war between human kind!

Ann Expert: There you go … interrupting me again! I've a good mind to punch you in the gob. Take that, horse face!

FIVE WEEKS LATER

Jeremy Axeman: Goood eevening. Just as we feared, the outbreaks of unpleasantness we reported a few weeks ago have now turned into non-stop violence everywhere. As a result, people are now calling these
terrible times, the Age of Metal and Blood. We're going over to the latest troublespot where Nora Weejanbod is cowering behind a huge heap of dead thralls.

Nora Weejanbod: This is Nora Weejanbod reporting from a battlefield somewhere in Midgard. It's horrible! The ground is red with the blood of mortals. I can see brother slaying brother, son slaying father and lots of other things that are all too far horrible for me to describe. Anyway, we'll show you those bits in slow motion later in the programme. Oh, oh, what can it all mean?

Jeremy Axeman: Search me Nora, I haven't the foggiest? And talking of fog, it's time to join our weather woman, Wynn Terdrawerson. She's got more bad news

Wynn Terdrawerson: I'm afraid I have, Jeremy. We're in for a cold snap. Well, more of a long term freeze-up, actually. If you were thinking of booking your summer hols, forget it! We aren't going to be having any summers, springs *or* autumns for quite some time to come! All of the worlds are going to be gripped by permanent winter and there will be nothing but ice storms and blizzards for the next three years. We've decided to call this big freeze, Fimbulvetr.

Jeremy Axeman: Ooh, cripes!

THREE YEARS LATER

Jeremy Axeman: Good evening and welcome to Bad Newsnight. Well, after wiping out most of the animals in Midgard – not to mention *stacks* of human beings! – Fimbulvetr, the dreadful three year long winter is finally over. But it seems that no sooner have we got rid of one problem than another one arrives. Now we've got constant darkness to put up with. Ann Expert's come into the studio to tell us what's going on! Ann, what in Midgard is happening?

Ann Expert: Well, Jeremy, our observers have noticed that the giantess Angrboda has been feeding up the wolves Skoll and Hati on the corpses of all the mortals killed during the Age of Blood and Metal. The wolves' extra rations have obviously given them lots of added energy. Not long ago they finally managed to catch up with Sun and Moon and gobble them up. Which is why we've decided to call this age of darkness, the Wolf Age!

Jeremy Axeman: So that's why I can't find me socks in the morning. Can't the gods do anything about it?

Ann Expert: It doesn't look like it. Since the arrival of this terrible darkness their magic is only operating at a mere fraction of its normal strength. We're really concerned about this loss of power and suspect it may to soon lead to some enormously big problems. We really do fear *the worst!*

Jeremy Axeman: Oh, surely not. Things are bound to get back to normal soon. I mean, they can't get any worse than they are now. *Can they?*

TWO WEEKS LATER

Familiar voice: ...and take the six eagles' eggs, a pinch of nutmeg and...

Anxious voice: We're interrupting Delia Myth's "Twenty Things To Do With A Frozen Horse" to bring you a news flash. A few minutes ago we received the disturbing news that Loki, the Trickster god, has broken free! He says that he is going to "Raise Hel"! Hel is said to be delighted and really looking forward to being up and about again. We're watching the situation very closely and will bring you more news as it happens. OK, back to Delia…

Delia Myth: …break the eggs into a container, your husband's war helmet will do…

Anxious Voice: Sorry about this Delia! It's *more* bad news. We've just heard that the wolf, Fenrir, has managed to snap Gleipnir, his chain. He was last seen heading in the direction of Jotunheim! Now – we'll return to Delia again…

Delia Myth: …then defrost the horse and simmer it for three days in a vat of…

Anxious Voice: I'm sorry, but we're going to have to interrupt this programme once more to bring you even more grim news on the rapidly worsening worlds situation. The world serpent, Jormungand, is now reported to be twitching and writhing in a most alarming

fashion. It looks like he might be about to leave the sea bed and join up with Fenrir and Hel. Niddhog, the dragon, is gnawing the roots of Yggdrasil as if he wants to bring the whole World Tree crashing down and hasn't a moment to lose. Great tremors are are already shaking all of the worlds and we've had reports of horrendous earthquakes in many regions. We also have more news on the Hel situation. Five minutes ago our underworld correspondent spotted her and the demon dog, Garm, emerging from a crack in the earth. They were followed by hordes of zombies. And finally, a great ship, made entirely from dead men's nails and absolutely packed with giants, has been spotted heading across the ocean from Jotunheim to the Plain of Vigrid. Bad Newsnight will bring you a full report on these and other deeply disturbing developments in an extended "Nine Worlds Crisis Special" later this evening. Now, we'll go back back to Delia. Oh? We can't! She's just died of starvation.

BAD NEWSNIGHT: NINE WORLDS CRISIS SPECIAL

Jeremy Axeman: Welcome. I'm standing on the Rainbow Bridge, just outside Asgard. You join me during what must be the most serious situation to have threatened the peace of the worlds since the wars between the gods back in the days following the Creation. A few moments ago Heimdall, the guardian of Bifrost, lifted his horn, Gjall, to his lips and blew a long and mournful note to warn the other gods of the terrible events that are unfolding below us as I speak. From up here on Bifrost we have got an excellent view of the Plain of Vigrid.

It is absolutely *swarming* with every variety of giant, zombie, monster and weird thing that you could possibly imagine. And they're all coming this way! These evil hordes are led by Loki, Fenris, Hel and Jormungand. Need I say more? With the distant and chilling chant of *"Bash the gods! Trash the gods! We are going to SMASH the gods!"* growing louder by the second, this is Jeremey Axeman handing you over to Nora Weejanbod, up in Valhalla.

Nora Weejanbod: Thanks, Jeremy! You join *me* amidst a scene of the most intense activity imaginable. Axes are being taken from walls, swords unsheathed and doors flung open by the dozen. The air is full of the sound of tramping feet and shouted orders. Above it all I can hear Gullinkambi, the alarm cock, crowing his lungs out. For what seems like ages, thousands of warriors have been marching out of Valhalla. As the first troops left the Hall of the Dead I caught sight of brave Thor and noble Odin at the head a great sea of bobbing helmets.

"This is the big one, isn't it, dad?" I heard Thor say grimly.

"Sure looks like it, son," replied Odin. "Best of luck, our kid!" And I saw him wink at Thor! Well, actually it was more of a *blink* than a wink, him having just the one eye. Nevertheless, a *very* touching moment! I'll return you to Jeremy now. He should be down on the Plain of Vigrid.

Jeremy Axeman: Yes, I am Nora. And I'm right in the thick of it! A full scale battle is raging all around me. Oi … mind that war axe! This must be the conflict to end all conflicts. As I speak, warriors from Valhalla, gods, giants and monsters are knocking the stuffing out of each other. Only minutes ago I witnessed the most terrible scrap between between Odin and Fenrir.

"Feeling lucky, dog's breath?" laughed Odin, as the two great enemies came face to face. Fenrir's only reply was a savage growl followed by a wag of his huge tail. Then he pounced! Odin grappled bravely but the slavering monster soon got the better of him and, opening its vast jaws, it swallowed him whole. One gulp and he was gone. Just like that! The horrible creature has just done an enormous burp and is now licking its bloodstained paws in an extremely self-satisfied and irritating manner. But just a mo'! What's this? It's Vidar, Odin's son. He's rushed at Fenrir and prised apart his jaws! Is he going to reach inside him and try and pull his dad out? No, he's actually ripping Fenrir completely in two. Nice one Vidar! Pity about your old man though! He was one of the best! OK, I'll hand you back to Nora now.

Nora Weejanbod: Thanks, Jeremy. I am now also on the battlefield and I'm watching Thor and Jormungand circling each other warily. Thor's just sneered contemptuously at Jormungand and said, "Make my day, snake!" And Jormungand's responded with some very unpleasant hissing! Oh, here they *go*! Thor's in first with a couple of blows from Mjollnir and Jormungand's thrashing and twisting like a crazy thing. Thor's now hammering away at him for all he's worth but the evil serpent's spraying great showers of deadly venom over him. Uurgh! I've just got a face full myself! It's *horrible*! Now they're *both* down. Thor has gone quite pale and is clutching his stomach while Jormungand is twitching and shuddering all over. It looks like they're done for. I'll just have a quick word with Thor. Thor, you took quite a drenching with deadly venom there, not to mention being horribly slashed by Jormungand's massive fangs. So! How do you *feeel*?

Thor: Uuuuurgh – ooaaor – haaaa – ummmph!

Nora Weejanbod: Well I never! Thor's died! And he didn't even answer *my* question. Well, at least nasty old Jormungand's dead too. I'll hand you back to Jeremy now. I'm actually not feeling too good myse—

Jeremy Axeman: Hello! Since I last spoke to you things have gone from bad to worse. Just minutes ago, I watched Heimdall and Loki kill each other horribly. Then moments after that I witnessed Tyr fatally plunge his sword into the Hel hound, Garm. But not before that devil dog had ripped out the god's *own* throat! Poor Tyr never did have much luck with dogs, did he?

This battle really is turning into a massacre of the worst kind. I have just received the sad news that my colleague, Nora Weejanbod, has died from severe facial poisoning. And I too, have taken a bite from a rabid zombie. The blood is spurting from a gaping hole in my neck as I speak. Uuurgh! Oh! Uh! There are thousands of twitching, steaming corpses everywhere and my head is filled with the ear splitting howls and moans of the dying.

In the distance I can see the fire giant, Surt, rushing around, flaming sword in hand, setting light to everything he can see. As he goes about his wicked business the individual fires are joining to form a huge inferno which has now spread so far that even the villages of Midgard and the palaces of Asgard and Jotunheim are being consumed by its flames.

I think this really must be … the end of the worlds as we know them! Everyone is dead! Gods, humans, giants, dwarves, monsters, everyone. Yes, all gone! Apart from me and my brave camera crew (who are also all fatally wounded!). My legs are wobbly and my vision is blurry. I am very weak. I have lost nearly all of my blood and think I will die quite soon. But wait! Who is *that*? Beneath the roots of Yggdrasil, the World Tree? Do I spy two tiny faces peeping out from its roots? I think I do! Can this be so? Could it be … *new life*? New hope? Or are my dimming eyes deceiving me? Everything is going dark. I am done for. This is (or was) Jeremy Axeman for Bad Newsnight, handing you over to … who knows what?

Footnote: The World Is Dead – Long Live The world! You'll be relieved to know that in the Viking legends, despite the fact that Ragnarok really did appear to devastate the nine worlds completely, things do eventually start up all over again. Light and warmth returned in the shape of the daughter the old Sun had given birth to just before she was eaten by Hati, the wolf. So it wasn't too long before things began growing again. People eventually returned as well. The two little faces peeping out from beneath Yggdrasil belonged to two humans beings called Lif and Lifthrasir. As soon as it was safe, they got really busy creating lots of new, little Lif(e)s.

Odin's son Vidar survived the disaster too, as did Thor's two strapping sons, Magni and Modi. Vili, one of the gods who had created the nine worlds in the first place, also survived. These remaining gods got together and set about creating a brand new heaven.

The best news of all was the release of Balder from Hel. Along with Nanna, he returned to join his fellow gods in the new world. His brother, Hod, also came back to life! Balder generously forgave him for so stupidly killing him and they became firm friends for evermore. And that was sort of fitting … because in this brave new world there was going to be no room for anger or hatred … or spiteful and unpleasant people. It really did look as though from now on, everyone in the new world could look forward to a bright new future and the wonderful prospect of spending the rest of their days in Peace, Happiness and Harmony (or maybe even in Milton Keynes?)

New world – New Aesir!

189

FANTASTIC FACTS 10: THE VIOLENT VIKINGS

With all those scenes of savage scrapping, death and destruction, the violent Vikings must have loved the legend of Ragnarok. They seemed to be completely mad about fighting and death and anything connected with it. Whether they were slaying foes, being bumped off themselves, making a sacrifice to a god, or organizing a spectacular send off for a dead comrade, they seemed to go completely over the top, *whatever* the gruesome occasion. Maybe they lived their whole lives convinced that every single move they ever made was being watched over by Odin and the other bloodthirsty gods. Perhaps they even thought that Odin and his god squad were like some sort of invisible selection committee in the sky, constantly dishing out points to the most violent and daring Vikings. Of course, if that was the case, the last thing they'd want to do was look like pathetic wimps in the eyes of those they worshipped! They'd be forever doing their best to show off their vocation for violence and their talent for toughness. It was their way of making sure they would finally be awarded the big prize that all self-respecting Viking warriors dreamed of and worked towards – their very own spot in Valhalla, the big cruelty club in the sky!

1 Fighting mad One of the best ways to get into Odin's good books was to become one of the one main death and destruction tornadoes known as "berserkers". As well as being the "know-all" god, Odin was the "beat-all god". His spirit was said to possess certain Viking warriors as they went into battle, instantly turning them into invincible and completely fearless fighting machines. These extremely stroppy individuals were given the name berserkers (or berserks) because they were said to wear the skins of bears when they went into battle. However, some historians seem to think they fought completely nude – in other words, in "bare skins". (In which case, where did they keep their spare ammo' and sandwiches?)

Once the berserkers had got themselves worked up into a proper paddy nothing short of a nuclear missile could stop them, and they would charge at the enemy uttering wild cries of hatred whilst biting the edge of their shields and foaming uncontrollably from the mouth. In other words, just like your average teacher coming into the classroom! Upon seeing them, their enemies would often flee in terror and then the berserkers would just have to be content with having a bit of a wrestle with any rocks or bushes that were stupid enough to be lying around the battlefield. Sometimes they

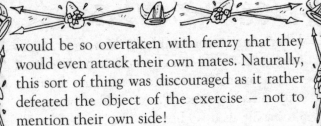

would be so overtaken with frenzy that they would even attack their own mates. Naturally, this sort of thing was discouraged as it rather defeated the object of the exercise – not to mention their own side!

2 Egil Skallagrimmson – "The right stuff"

The Viking warrior, Egil Skallagrimmson may well have held the record for being the youngest berserker ever, after making a really early start to his well-known career of murder and mayhem. It was reported that when Egil was only six years old, he had a bit of a disagreement with a playmate during a ball game so he immediately beat him to death with his bat. And it didn't stop there! When various servants and relatives came to see what all the fuss was about, the little tike got stuck into them and bumped off seven of them too! Rather than slapping his legs or sending him up to his bedroom without his tea, his mum was really impressed with her lad's first outbreak of homicidal rage and proudly said that he was made "*of Viking stuff*". She also said that as soon as he was old enough he should get out and "hew a man in twain". Or, to put it another way, she thought it was about time he went out chopping (people!). So, at the ripe young age of twelve, young Egil was given his very own longship and team of cold-blooded

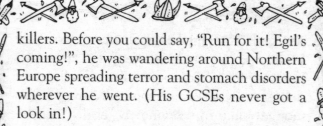

killers. Before you could say, "Run for it! Egil's coming!", he was wandering around Northern Europe spreading terror and stomach disorders wherever he went. (His GCSEs never got a look in!)

3 Nothing to get into a flap about Rather than speeding their enemies on their way to the next world with a gentle tap on the bonce, the Vikings varied their violence by dreaming up all sorts of spectacular and horrible tortures. After all, if you are a professional spreader of terror and mayhem, you might as well do it as imaginatively and creatively as you possibly can. That way, you make sure that a "don't mess with the Vikings!" message strikes home wherever you rampage. So reader, if you've just eaten your breakfast or are a member of a royal family, definitely *don't* read this next bit!

In AD 867, after a bit of a dust-up with the English, some Danish Vikings captured an English ruler called King Ella Of Northumbria. As a way of teaching him a lesson he'd never forget, they broke open his rib cage and pulled his lungs out through the hole they'd made in his back ... so that they sort of just "dangled" behind him. (Still reading? You *are* a glutton for punishment, aren't you!) The poor king's dying breaths caused the lungs to flap about rather pathetically, like a pair of bird's wings.

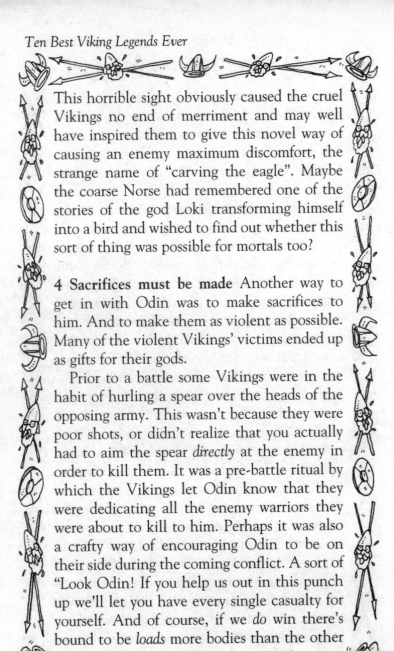

This horrible sight obviously caused the cruel Vikings no end of merriment and may well have inspired them to give this novel way of causing an enemy maximum discomfort, the strange name of "carving the eagle". Maybe the coarse Norse had remembered one of the stories of the god Loki transforming himself into a bird and wished to find out whether this sort of thing was possible for mortals too?

4 Sacrifices must be made Another way to get in with Odin was to make sacrifices to him. And to make them as violent as possible. Many of the violent Vikings' victims ended up as gifts for their gods.

Prior to a battle some Vikings were in the habit of hurling a spear over the heads of the opposing army. This wasn't because they were poor shots, or didn't realize that you actually had to aim the spear *directly* at the enemy in order to kill them. It was a pre-battle ritual by which the Vikings let Odin know that they were dedicating all the enemy warriors they were about to kill to him. Perhaps it was also a crafty way of encouraging Odin to be on their side during the coming conflict. A sort of "Look Odin! If you help us out in this punch up we'll let you have every single casualty for yourself. And of course, if we *do* win there's bound to be *loads* more bodies than the other

lot could give you!"

Odin was said to have complete control over the outcomes of all battles.

(So why fight them? He could just tell the Vikings who was going to win and they could all go home none the worse for wear!) The night before one battle between two equally ferocious bands of warriors, Odin's wife Frigg asked him who he would be choosing as the winners. Odin said it would be the army he first saw when he opened his eyes next morning. Frigg wasn't too keen on the army that Odin was facing at the time so while he was asleep she turned his bed around. And of course, her favourites won!

5 Hang about! – We're going to have to make even more sacrifices The violent Vikings were obviously really impressed with Odin's self-hanging session which gave him so much knowledge. Maybe they quite fancied having a go at this for themselves, perhaps as way of saying, "That was a great trick you pulled back there in the woods Odin! And we're going to copy it!" However, they weren't stupid. They realized that this way of honouring their favourite god would probably leave them dead … rather than just dead clever! So they went for the easy option and strung up lots of other people instead. When they attacked Nantes in

Northern France in AD 842 they slaughtered the entire population, then dangled them from trees around the city. Sadly though, none of the French people ended up any the wiser!

6 I'm sorry, but even more sacrifices must be made ... including you, pal! The violent Vikings weren't just content with bumping off their enemies as sacrifices to Odin. They also killed people and animals from their own clans and groups. Their favourite way of doing this was ritually to hang them and stab them at the same time. Perhaps it was less painful this way? Maybe one lot of agony sort of cancelled out the other? Quite a few of the unlucky people and animals who died in this way were dumped in the peat bogs and marshy pools that are found in parts of Sweden and Denmark. The peat acted as a preservative and prevented the bodies from decomposing. During recent times lots of the victims have been dug up looking more or less as they did when they were bunged in the bogs. One of the most famous is a man who was found in a bog at Tollund in Denmark with the rope that was used to strangle him still around his neck and a sort of tranquil, "Well I never, I'm just about to become a gift for a top god! Just wait until I tell the lads down the pub about this!" expression on his face.

7 A right royal send-off! Some Vikings were always looking for an excuse to bump someone off in honour of their number one god. Even if it meant betraying their local number one human. Starkad, one of King Vikar's Viking warriors, was said to be a favourite of Odin. One day King Vikar's fleet of ships became becalmed at sea. A sacrifice would have to be made to Odin so that he'd whip up some wind to get the ships moving again. Lots were drawn to decide who and King Vikar's name came up for the chop! "Oower!" thought his men, "This is a bit tricky. Perhaps we'll sleep on it!" During the night, Odin nipped down from Asgard and said something like, "You really are my favourite warrior Starkad. Oh, and by the way, I couldn't half do with that King Vikar as a sacrifice. (Nudge, nudge, wink, wink!)" And then he handed him a spear that looked just like a reed. In the meantime King Vikar's men had decided that, rather than killing their king, they would just *pretend* to sacrifice him. Spotting his opportunity, Starkad said, "Leave that to me chaps. I'll sort it!" He then wrapped some soft calf guts around the king's neck, tied their other end to a twig, then made him stand on a log ready for the "execution". Unfortunately for King Vikar, the moment Starkad kicked away the log, the guts magically turned into a rope, the twig became

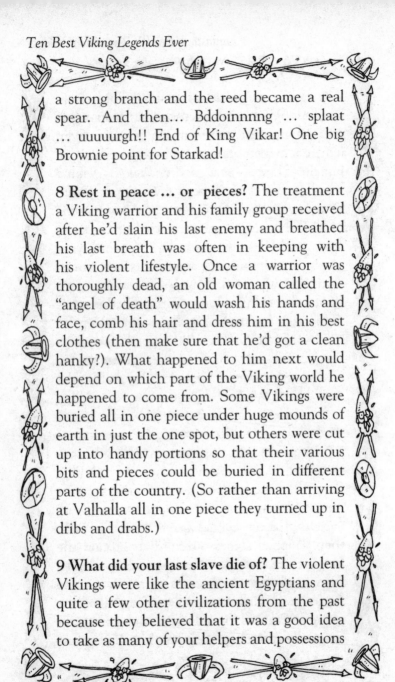

a strong branch and the reed became a real spear. And then... Bddoinnnng ... splaat ... uuuuurgh!! End of King Vikar! One big Brownie point for Starkad!

8 Rest in peace ... or pieces? The treatment a Viking warrior and his family group received after he'd slain his last enemy and breathed his last breath was often in keeping with his violent lifestyle. Once a warrior was thoroughly dead, an old woman called the "angel of death" would wash his hands and face, comb his hair and dress him in his best clothes (then make sure that he'd got a clean hanky?). What happened to him next would depend on which part of the Viking world he happened to come from. Some Vikings were buried all in one piece under huge mounds of earth in just the one spot, but others were cut up into handy portions so that their various bits and pieces could be buried in different parts of the country. (So rather than arriving at Valhalla all in one piece they turned up in dribs and drabs.)

9 What did your last slave die of? The violent Vikings were like the ancient Egyptians and quite a few other civilizations from the past because they believed that it was a good idea to take as many of your helpers and possessions into the next world as you possibly could (rather than having to shop for them when you got there). So, if you happened to be a female slave of a top Viking warrior who had just died, there was a good chance you would be joining him in his burial chamber – even if you actually hadn't got round to dying yourself! A slave girl who was going to be buried (or burned) along with her Viking employer would first be wined and dined and generally made a fuss of. Perhaps so she wouldn't hold a grudge against all the other Vikings in view of what they were about to do to her? When she was well and truly sozzled she would be made to lie down next to her boss's body. Then, with the other warrors giving her a cheerful send-off by merrily beating on their shields, the "angel of death" (yes, *her* again!) would thrust a dagger into the slave girl's heart until she was well and truly dead.

Top Vikings were buried with their weapons, horses, carts, sledges, oxen, chests of clothes, spare cloak, bed, and anything else they thought they'd need for a really comfy and convenient after-life. Oak buckets filled with snacks like apples and walnuts were also put in some graves – maybe so they wouldn't get peckish or die of starvation on their journey to the next world? Viking chiefs were often buried with their favourite ships too. The big boats provided a handy storage unit for all the other bits and bobs including the chief himself. The graves for these ship burials were enormous, often as long as 60 metres and almost as wide again. When modern archaeologists dig up the site of a Viking ship burial it usually means they're going to get their hands on some really interesting artefacts so they get very excited (but the Vikings themselves remain completely cool).

10 The hot favourite If Viking chiefs didn't fancy the idea of being buried inside their boats then nibbled by the worms, a spectacular and violent alternative way for them to say cheerio to their pals was to be *burned* inside their boats, then nibbled by the *fish*! The dead Viking who had chosen this way to make his exit from the world was put aboard his best ship along with all his favourite possessions and his wife and slave girls. (If they weren't already dead they soon would be!) The ship would be sent out to sea and set on fire by his nearest relative – who, if they had any sense, would make sure they weren't actually aboard it at the time.

After his bit of bad luck with the mistletoe, the god Balder was given a ship-burning funeral by the other gods. Of course, being the funeral

of a Viking god, Balder's send-off didn't go smoothly. It was interrupted by an incident of horrible violence! (Surprised? No, of course you aren't!) As the gods stood watching Balder's blazing funeral ship floating out to sea, a dwarf called Lit happened to jog along the beach in front of them in a most disrespectful way. Thor was so annoyed by this that he gave Lit a boot up the backside which caused the little bloke to fly through the air like a rugby ball. The poor mite landed right on the flaming funeral boat alongside Balder and his wife Nanna and moments later he was burned to death. So the funeral boat got 'lit' twice!

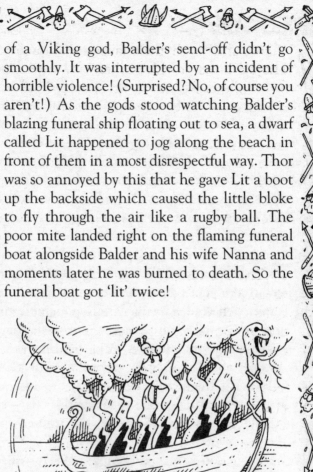

EPILOGUE

You may find it hard to believe, but, year by year, decade by decade and century by century, the warlike, action-loving Vikings actually began to lose interest in top rootin' tootin' heroes like Thor and Odin, and towards the end of the tenth century a new set of stories and characters began to replace these old ones. Rather than being told by skalds and bards, these new tales were put about by story-tellers known as missionaries and were about the exploits of a new hero called Jesus. And rather than being thrilling tales of two-fisted superheroes who solved problems by walloping first and asking questions afterwards, these calmer and more thoughtful "parables" suggested that a "Let's all try and be a bit nicer to each other" approach to life was generally preferable to the old "Find 'em … frash 'em … forget 'em!" style that had been so popular in the old days. And the thing that was really radical about these new stories and the religion that went with them was the idea that – instead of heaven being bursting at the seams with gods – there was actually only one of them, i.e. the true Christian one!

For some reason – maybe because they realised the futility of forever feuding and fighting? – the "new Norse" eventually got quite used to these ideas, abandoned their old gods and quite a few of their warlike ways, and began to worship the new one. By the end of the eleventh century they were busy building newfangled wooden Christian churches as they looked forward to a bright new future consisting almost entirely of peaceful occupations like farming and fishing (and building incredibly safe motor cars). Nevertheless old habits die hard and, even a thousand years on, you can still see Viking warriors (or Hell's Angels as they're now known) charging around Scandinavia on their enormous motorbikes as they no doubt race to their local bookshops to grab the latest version of the exploits of Thor and Odin … certain in the knowledge that those ancient Viking legends never fail to thrill!

IF YOU LIKE THIS, YOU MIGHT LIKE...

100% HORRIBLE

SIR LANCE-A-LOT AT YOUR SERVICE!

10 BEST ARThurian LeGends EVER!

Margaret Simpson

100% HORRIBLE

10 BEST GREEK LEGENDS EVER!

ANOTHER BAD HAIR DAY...

TROY

Terry Deary

Author of Horrible Histories

HE'S A
BONE IDOL!

100%
HORRIBLE

10 BEST SHAKESPEARE STORIES EVER!

Terry Deary
Author of Horrible Histories